The Book of Adam and Eve

The Conflict of Adam and Eve with Satan

Solomon C. Malan

TABLE OF CONTENTS

Chapter I - The crystal sea, God commands Adam, expelled from Eden, to live in the Cave of Treasures.

1 On the third day, God planted the garden in the east of the earth, on the border of the world eastward, beyond which, towards the sun-rising, one finds nothing but water, that encompasses the whole world, and reaches to the borders of heaven.

2 And to the north of the garden there is a sea of water, clear and pure to the taste, unlike anything else; so that, through the clearness thereof, one may look into the depths of the earth.

3 And when a man washes himself in it, he becomes clean of the cleanness thereof, and white of its whiteness—even if he were dark.

4 And God created that sea of his own good pleasure, for He knew what would come of the man He would make; so that after he had left the garden, on account of his transgression, men should be born in the earth. Among them are righteous ones who will die, whose souls God would raise at the last day; when all of them will return to their flesh, bathe in the water of that sea, and repent of their sins.

5 But when God made Adam go out of the garden, He did not place him on the border of it northward. This was so that he and Eve would not be able to go near to the sea of water where they could wash themselves in it, be cleansed from their sins, erase the transgression they had committed, and be no longer reminded of it in the thought of their punishment.

6 As to the southern side of the garden, God did not want Adam to live there either; because, when the wind blew from the north, it would bring him, on that southern side, the delicious smell of the trees of the garden.

7 Wherefore God did not put Adam there. This was so that he would not be able to smell the sweet smell of those trees, forget his transgression, and find consolation for what he had done by taking delight in the smell of the trees and yet not be cleansed from his transgression.

8 Again, also, because God is merciful and of great pity, and governs all things in a way that He alone knows—He made our father Adam live in the western border of the garden, because on that side the earth is very broad.

9 And God commanded him to live there in a cave in a rock—the Cave of Treasures below the garden.

Chapter II - Adam and Eve faint when they leave the Garden. God sends His Word to encourage them.

1 But when our father Adam, and Eve, went out of the garden, they walked the ground on their feet, not knowing they were walking.

2 And when they came to the opening of the gate of the garden, and saw the broad earth spread before them, covered with stones large and small, and with sand, they feared and trembled, and fell on their faces, from the fear that came over them; and they were as dead.

3 Because—whereas until this time they had been in the garden land, beautifully planted with all manner of trees—they now saw themselves, in a strange land, which they knew not, and had never seen.

4 And because, when they were in the garden they were filled with the grace of a bright nature, and they had not hearts turned toward earthly things.

5 Therefore God had pity on them; and when He saw them fallen before the gate of the garden, He sent His Word to our father, Adam and Eve, and raised them from their fallen state.

Chapter III - Concerning the promise of the great five and a half days.

1 God said to Adam, "I have ordained on this earth days and years, and you and your descendants shall live and walk in them, until the days and years are fulfilled; when I shall send the Word that created you, and against which you have transgressed, the Word that made you come out of the garden, and that raised you when you were fallen.

2 Yes, the Word that will again save you when the five and a half days are fulfilled."

3 But when Adam heard these words from God, and of the great five and a half days, he did not understand the meaning of them.

4 For Adam was thinking there would be only five and a half days for him until the end of the world.

5 And Adam cried, and prayed to God to explain it to him.

6 Then God in his mercy for Adam who was made after His own image and likeness, explained to him, that these were 5,000 and 500 years; and how One would then come and save him and his descendants.

7 But before that, God had made this covenant with our father, Adam, in the same terms, before he came out of the garden, when he was by the tree where Eve took of the fruit and gave it to him to eat.

8 Because, when our father Adam came out of the garden, he passed by that tree, and saw how God had changed the appearance of it into another form, and how it shriveled.

9 And as Adam went to it he feared, trembled and fell down; but God in His mercy lifted him up, and then made this covenant with him.

10 And again, when Adam was by the gate of the garden, and saw the cherub with a sword of flashing fire in his hand, and the cherub grew angry and frowned at him, both Adam and

Eve became afraid of him, and thought he meant to put them to death. So they fell on their faces, trembled with fear.

11 But he had pity on them, and showed them mercy; and turning from them went up to heaven, and prayed to the Lord, and said;—

12 "Lord, You sent me to watch at the gate of the garden, with a sword of fire.

13 But when Your servants, Adam and Eve, saw me, they fell on their faces, and were as dead. O my Lord, what shall we do to Your servants?"

14 Then God had pity on them, and showed them mercy, and sent His Angel to keep the garden.

15 And the Word of the Lord came to Adam and Eve, and raised them up.

16 And the Lord said to Adam, "I told you that at the end of the five and a half days, I will send my Word and save you.

17 Strengthen your heart, therefore, and stay in the Cave of Treasures, of which I have before spoken to you."

18 And when Adam heard this Word from God, he was comforted with that which God had told him. For He had told him how He would save him.

Chapter IV - Adam mourns over the changed conditions. Adam and Eve enter the Cave of Treasures.

1 But Adam and Eve cried for having come out of the garden, their first home.

2 And indeed, when Adam looked at his flesh, that was altered, he cried bitterly, he and Eve, over what they had done. And they walked and went gently down into the Cave of Treasures.

3 And as they came to it, Adam cried over himself and said to Eve, "Look at this cave that is to be our prison in this world, and a place of punishment!

4 What is it compared with the garden? What is its narrowness compared with the space of the other?

5 What is this rock, by the side of those groves? What is the gloom of this cavern, compared with the light of the garden?

6 What is this overhanging ledge of rock to shelter us, compared with the mercy of the Lord that overshadowed us?

7 What is the soil of this cave compared with the garden land? This earth, strewed with stones; and that, planted with delicious fruit trees?"

8 And Adam said to Eve, "Look at your eyes, and at mine, which before beheld angels praising in heaven; and they too, without ceasing.

9 But now we do not see as we did; our eyes have become of flesh; they cannot see like they used to see before."

10 Adam said again to Eve, "What is our body today, compared to what it was in former days, when we lived in the garden?"

11 After this, Adam did not want to enter the cave, under the overhanging rock; nor would he ever want to enter it.

12 But he bowed to God's orders; and said to himself, "Unless I enter the cave, I shall again be a transgressor."

Chapter V - Eve makes a noble and emotional intercession, taking the blame on herself.

1 Then Adam and Eve entered the cave, and stood praying, in their own tongue, unknown to us, but which they knew well.

2 And as they prayed, Adam raised his eyes and saw the rock and the roof of the cave that covered him overhead. This prevented him from seeing either heaven or God's creatures. So he cried and beat his chest hard, until he dropped, and was as dead.

3 And Eve sat crying; for she believed he was dead.

4 Then she got up, spread her hands toward God, appealing to Him for mercy and pity, and said, "O God, forgive me my sin, the sin which I committed, and don't remember it against me.

5 For I alone caused Your servant to fall from the garden into this condemned land; from light into this darkness; and from the house of joy into this prison.

6 O God, look at this Your servant fallen in this manner, and bring him back to life, that he may cry and repent of his transgression which he committed through me.

7 Don't take away his soul right now; but let him live that he may stand after the measure of his repentance, and do Your will, as before his death.

8 But if You do not bring him back to life, then, O God, take away my own soul, that I be like him, and leave me not in this dungeon, one and alone; for I could not stand alone in this world, but with him only.

9 For You, O God, caused him to fall asleep, and took a bone from his side, and restored the flesh in the place of it, by Your divine power.

10 And You took me, the bone, and make me a woman, bright like him, with heart, reason, and speech; and in flesh, like to his own; and You made me after the likeness of his looks, by Your mercy and power.

11 O Lord, I and he are one, and You, O God, are our Creator, You are He who made us both in one day.

12 Therefore, O God, give him life, that he may be with me in this strange land, while we live in it on account of our transgression.

13 But if You will not give him life, then take me, even me, like him; that we both may die the same day."

14 And Eve cried bitterly, and fell on our father Adam; from her great sorrow.

Chapter VI - God's reprimand to Adam and Eve in which he points out how and why they sinned.

1 But God looked at them; for they had killed themselves through great grief.

2 But He decided to raise them and comfort them.

3 He, therefore, sent His Word to them; that they should stand and be raised immediately.

4 And the Lord said to Adam and Eve, "You transgressed of your own free will, until you came out of the garden in which I had placed you.

5 Of your own free will have you transgressed through your desire for divinity, greatness, and an exalted state, such as I have; so that I deprived you of the bright nature in which you then were, and I made you come out of the garden to this land, rough and full of trouble.

6 If only you had not transgressed My commandment and had kept My law, and had not eaten of the fruit of the tree which I told you not to come near! And there were fruit trees in the garden better than that one.

7 But the wicked Satan did not keep his faith and had no good intent towards Me, that although I had created him, he considered Me to be useless, and sought the Godhead for himself; for this I hurled him down from heaven so that he could not remain in his first estate—it was he who made the tree appear pleasant in your eyes, until you ate of it, by believing his words.

8 Thus have you transgressed My commandment, and therefore I have brought on you all these sorrows.

9 For I am God the Creator, who, when I created My creatures, did not intend to destroy them. But after they had sorely roused My anger, I punished them with grievous plagues, until they repent.

10 But, if on the contrary, they still continue hardened in their transgression, they shall be under a curse forever."

Chapter VII - The beasts are appeased.

1 When Adam and Eve heard these words from God, they cried and sobbed yet more; but they strengthened their hearts in God, because they now felt that the Lord was to them like a father and a mother; and for this very reason, they cried before Him, and sought mercy from Him.

2 Then God had pity on them, and said: "O Adam, I have made My covenant with you, and I will not turn from it; neither will I let you return to the garden, until My covenant of the great five and a half days is fulfilled."

3 Then Adam said to God, "O Lord, You created us, and made us fit to be in the garden; and before I transgressed, You made all beasts come to me, that I should name them.

4 Your grace was then on me; and I named every one according to Your mind; and you made them all subject to me.

5 But now, O Lord God, that I have transgressed Your commandment, all beasts will rise against me and will devour me, and Eve Your handmaid; and will cut off our life from the face of the earth.

6 I therefore beg you, O God, that since You have made us come out of the garden, and have made us be in a strange land, You will not let the beasts hurt us."

7 When the Lord heard these words from Adam, He had pity on him, and felt that he had truly said that the beasts of the field would rise and devour him and Eve, because He, the Lord, was angry with the two of them on account of their transgressions.

8 Then God commanded the beasts, and the birds, and all that moves on the earth, to come to Adam and to be familiar with him, and not to trouble him and Eve; nor yet any of the good and righteous among their offspring.

9 Then all the beasts paid homage to Adam, according to the commandment of God; except the serpent, against which God was angry. It did not come to Adam, with the beasts.

Chapter VIII - The "Bright Nature" of man is taken away.

1 Then Adam cried and said, "O God, when we lived in the garden, and our hearts were lifted up, we saw the angels that sang praises in heaven, but now we can't see like we used to; no, when we entered the cave, all creation became hidden from us."

2 Then God the Lord said to Adam, "When you were under subjection to Me, you had a bright nature within you, and for that reason could you see things far away. But after your transgression your bright nature was withdrawn from you; and it was not left to you to see things far away, but only near at hand; after the ability of the flesh; for it is brutish."

3 When Adam and Eve had heard these words from God, they went their way; praising and worshipping Him with a sorrowful heart.

4 And God ceased to commune with them.

Chapter IX - Water from the Tree of Life. Adam and Eve near drowning.

1 Then Adam and Eve came out of the Cave of Treasures, and went near to the garden gate, and there they stood to look at it, and cried for having come away from it.

2 And Adam and Eve went from before the gate of the garden to the southern side of it, and found there the water that watered the garden, from the root of the Tree of Life, and that split itself from there into four rivers over the earth.

3 Then they came and went near to that water, and looked at it; and saw that it was the water that came forth from under the root of the Tree of Life in the garden.

4 And Adam cried and wailed, and beat his chest, for being severed from the garden; and said to Eve:—

5 "Why have you brought on me, on yourself, and on our descendants, so many of these plagues and punishments?"

6 And Eve said to him, "What is it you have seen that has caused you to cry and to speak to me in this manner?"

7 And he said to Eve, "Do you not see this water that was with us in the garden, that watered the trees of the garden, and flowed out from there?

8 And we, when we were in the garden, did not care about it; but since we came to this strange land, we love it, and turn it to use for our body."

9 But when Eve heard these words from him, she cried; and from the soreness of their crying, they fell into that water; and would have put an end to themselves in it, so as never again to return and behold the creation; for when they looked at the work of creation, they felt they must put an end to themselves.

Chapter X - Their bodies need water after they leave the garden.

1 Then God, merciful and gracious, looked at them thus lying in the water, and close to death, and sent an angel, who brought them out of the water, and laid them on the seashore as dead.

2 Then the angel went up to God, was welcome, and said, "O God, Your creatures have breathed their last."

3 Then God sent His Word to Adam and Eve, who raised them from their death.

4 And Adam said, after he was raised, "O God, while we were in the garden we did not require, or care for this water; but since we came to this land we cannot do without it."

5 Then God said to Adam, "While you were under My command and were a bright angel, you knew not this water.

6 But now that you have transgressed My commandment, you can not do without water, wherein to wash your body and make it grow; for it is now like that of beasts, and is in want of water."

7 When Adam and Eve heard these words from God, they cried a bitter cry; and Adam entreated God to let him return into the garden, and look at it a second time.

8 But God said to Adam, "I have made you a promise; when that promise is fulfilled, I will bring you back into the garden, you and your righteous descendants."

9 And God ceased to commune with Adam.

Chapter XI - A recollection of the glorious days in the Garden.

1 Then Adam and Eve felt themselves burning with thirst, and heat, and sorrow.

2 And Adam said to Eve, "We shall not drink of this water, even if we were to die. O Eve, when this water comes into our inner parts, it will increase our punishments and that of our descendants."

3 Both Adam and Eve then went away from the water, and drank none of it at all; but came and entered the Cave of Treasures.

4 But when in it Adam could not see Eve; he only heard the noise she made. Neither could she see Adam, but heard the noise he made.

5 Then Adam cried, in deep affliction, and beat his chest; and he got up and said to Eve, "Where are you?"

6 And she said to him, "Look, I am standing in this darkness."

7 He then said to her, "Remember the bright nature in which we lived, when we lived in the garden!

8 O Eve! Remember the glory that rested on us in the garden. O Eve! Remember the trees that overshadowed us in the garden while we moved among them.

9 O Eve! Remember that while we were in the garden, we knew neither night nor day. Think of the Tree of Life, from below which flowed the water, and that shed lustre over us! Remember, O Eve, the garden land, and the brightness thereof!

10 Think, oh think of that garden in which was no darkness, while we lived in it.

11 Whereas no sooner did we come into this Cave of Treasures than darkness surrounded us all around; until we can no longer see each other; and all the pleasure of this life has come to an end."

Chapter XII - How darkness came between Adam and Eve.

1 Then Adam beat his chest, he and Eve, and they mourned the whole night until the crack of dawn, and they sighed over the length of the night in Miyazia.

2 And Adam beat himself, and threw himself on the ground in the cave, from bitter grief, and because of the darkness, and lay there as dead.

3 But Eve heard the noise he made in falling on the ground. And she felt about for him with her hands, and found him like a corpse.

4 Then she was afraid, speechless, and remained by him.

5 But the merciful Lord looked on the death of Adam, and on Eve's silence from fear of the darkness.

6 And the Word of God came to Adam and raised him from his death, and opened Eve's mouth that she might speak.

7 Then Adam stood up in the cave and said, "O God, why has light departed from us, and darkness covered us? Why did you leave us in this long darkness? Why do you plague us like this?

8 And this darkness, O Lord, where was it before it covered us? It is because of this that we cannot see each other.

9 For so long as we were in the garden, we neither saw nor even knew what darkness is. I was not hidden from Eve, neither was she hidden from me, until now that she cannot see me; and no darkness came over us to separate us from each other.

10 But she and I were both in one bright light. I saw her and she saw me. Yet now since we came into this cave, darkness has covered us, and separated us from each other, so that I do not see her, and she does not see me.

11 O Lord, will You then plague us with this darkness?"

Chapter XIII - The fall of Adam. Why night and day were created.

1 Then when God, who is merciful and full of pity, heard Adam's voice, He said to him:—

2 "O Adam, so long as the good angel was obedient to Me, a bright light rested on him and on his hosts.

3 But when he transgressed My commandment, I deprived him of that bright nature, and he became dark.

4 And when he was in the heavens, in the realms of light, he knew nothing of darkness.

5 But he transgressed, and I made him fall from the heaven onto the earth; and it was this darkness that came over him.

6 And on you, O Adam, while in My garden and obedient to Me, did that bright light rest also.

7 But when I heard of your transgression, I deprived you of that bright light. Yet, of My mercy, I did not turn you into darkness, but I made you your body of flesh, over which I spread this skin, in order that it may bear cold and heat.

8 If I had let My wrath fall heavily on you, I should have destroyed you; and had I turned you into darkness, it would have been as if I had killed you.

9 But in My mercy, I have made you as you are; when you transgressed My commandment, O Adam, I drove you from the garden, and made you come forth into this land; and commanded you to live in this cave; and darkness covered you, as it did over him who transgressed My commandment.

10 Thus, O Adam, has this night deceived you. It is not to last forever; but is only of twelve hours; when it is over, daylight will return.

11 Sigh not, therefore, neither be moved; and say not in your heart that this darkness is long and drags on wearily; and say not in your heart that I plague you with it.

12 Strengthen your heart, and be not afraid. This darkness is not a punishment. But, O Adam, I have made the day, and have placed the sun in it to give light; in order that you and your children should do your work.

13 For I knew you would sin and transgress, and come out into this land. Yet I wouldn't force you, nor be heard over you, nor shut up; nor doom you through your fall; nor

through your coming out from light into darkness; nor yet through your coming from the garden into this land.

14 For I made you of the light; and I willed to bring out children of light from you and like to you.

15 But you did not keep My commandment one day; until I had finished the creation and blessed everything in it.

16 Then, concerning the tree, I commanded you not to eat of it. Yet I knew that Satan, who deceived himself, would also deceive you.

17 So I made known to you by means of the tree, not to come near him. And I told you not to eat of the fruit thereof, nor to taste of it, nor yet to sit under it, nor to yield to it.

18 Had I not been and spoken to you, O Adam, concerning the tree, and had I left you without a commandment, and you had sinned—it would have been an offence on My part, for not having given you any order; you would turn around and blame Me for it.

19 But I commanded you, and warned you, and you fell. So that My creatures cannot blame Me; but the blame rests on them alone.

20 And, O Adam, I have made the day so that you and your descendants can work and toil in it. And I have made the night for them to rest in it from their work; and for the beasts of the field to go forth by night and look for their food.

21 But little of darkness now remains, O Adam, and daylight will soon appear."

Chapter XIV - The earliest prophesy of the coming of Christ.

1 Then Adam said to God: "O Lord, take You my soul, and let me not see this gloom any more; or remove me to some place where there is no darkness."

2 But God the Lord said to Adam, "Indeed I say to you, this darkness will pass from you, every day I have determined for you, until the fulfillment of My covenant; when I will save you and bring you back again into the garden, into the house of light you long for, in which there is no darkness*. I will bring you to it—in the kingdom of heaven."

3 Again said God to Adam, "All this misery that you have been made to take on yourself because of your transgression, will not free you from the hand of Satan, and will not save you.

4 But I will. When I shall come down from heaven, and shall become flesh of your descendants, and take on Myself the infirmity from which you suffer, then the darkness that covered you in this cave shall cover Me in the grave, when I am in the flesh of your descendants.

5 And I, who am without years, shall be subject to the reckoning of years, of times, of months, and of days, and I shall be reckoned as one of the sons of men, in order to save you."

6 And God ceased to commune with Adam.

* Reference: John 12:46

Chapter XV - Adam and Eve grieve over the suffering of God to save them from their sins.

1 Then Adam and Eve cried and sorrowed by reason of God's word to them, that they should not return to the garden until the fulfillment of the days decreed on them; but mostly because God had told them that He should suffer for their salvation.

Chapter XVI - The first sunrise. Adam and Eve think it is a fire coming to burn them.

1 After this, Adam and Eve continued to stand in the cave, praying and crying, until the morning dawned on them.

2 And when they saw the light returned to them, they retrained from fear, and strengthened their hearts.

3 Then Adam began to come out of the cave. And when he came to the mouth of it, and stood and turned his face towards the east, and saw the sunrise in glowing rays, and felt the heat thereof on his body, he was afraid of it, and thought in his heart that this flame came forth to plague him.

4 He then cried and beat his chest, then he fell on the ground on his face and made his request, saying:—

5 "O Lord, plague me not, neither consume me, nor yet take away my life from the earth."

6 For he thought the sun was God.

7 Because while he was in the garden and heard the voice of God and the sound He made in the garden, and feared Him, Adam never saw the brilliant light of the sun, neither did its flaming heat touch his body.

8 Therefore he was afraid of the sun when flaming rays of it reached him. He thought God meant to plague him therewith all the days He had decreed for him.

9 For Adam also said in his thoughts, as God did not plague us with darkness, behold, He has caused this sun to rise and to plague us with burning heat.

10 But while he was thinking like this in his heart, the Word of God came to him and said:—

11 "O Adam, get up on your feet. This sun is not God; but it has been created to give light by day, of which I spoke to you in the cave saying, 'that the dawn would come, and there would be light by day.'

12 But I am God who comforted you in the night."

13 And God ceased to commune with Adam.

Chapter XVII - The Chapter of the Serpent.

1 The Adam and Eve came out at the mouth of the cave, and went towards the garden.

2 But as they went near it, before the western gate, from which Satan came when he deceived Adam and Eve, they found the serpent that became Satan coming at the gate, and sorrowfully licking the dust, and wiggling on its breast on the ground, by reason of the curse that fell on it from God.

3 And whereas before the serpent was the most exalted of all beasts, now it was changed and become slippery, and the meanest of them all, and it crept on its breast and went on its belly.

4 And whereas it was the fairest of all beasts, it had been changed, and was become the ugliest of them all. Instead of feeding on the best food, now it turned to eat the dust. Instead of living, as before, in the best places, now it lived in the dust.

5 And, whereas it had been the most beautiful of all beasts, all of which stood dumb at its beauty, it was now abhorred of them.

6 And, again, whereas it lived in one beautiful home, to which all other animals came from elsewhere; and where it drank, they drank also of the same; now, after it had become venomous, by reason of God's curse, all beasts fled from its home, and would not drink of the water it drank; but fled from it.

Chapter XVIII - The mortal combat with the serpent.

1 When the accursed serpent saw Adam and Eve, it swelled its head, stood on its tail, and with eyes blood-red, acted like it would kill them.

2 It made straight for Eve, and ran after her; while Adam standing by, cried because he had no stick in his hand with which to hit the serpent, and did not know how to put it to death.

3 But with a heart burning for Eve, Adam approached the serpent, and held it by the tail; when it turned towards him and said to him:—

4 "O Adam, because of you and of Eve, I am slippery, and go on my belly." Then with its great strength, it threw down Adam and Eve and squeezed them, and tried to kill them.

5 But God sent an angel who threw the serpent away from them, and raised them up.

6 Then the Word of God came to the serpent, and said to it, "The first time I made you slick, and made you to go on your belly; but I did not deprive you of speech.

7 This time, however, you will be mute, and you and your race will speak no more; because, the first time My creatures were ruined because of you, and this time you tried to kill them."

8 Then the serpent was struck mute, and was no longer able to speak.

9 And a wind blew down from heaven by the command of God and carried away the serpent from Adam and Eve, and threw it on the seashore where it landed in India.

Chapter XIX - Beasts made subject to Adam.

1 But Adam and Eve cried before God. And Adam said to Him:—

2 "O Lord, when I was in the cave, I said this to you, my Lord, the beasts of the field would rise and devour me, and cut off my life from the earth."

3 Then Adam, because of what had happened to him, beat his chest and fell on the ground like a corpse. Then the Word of God came to him, who raised him, and said to him,

4 "O Adam, not one of these beasts will be able to hurt you; because I have made the beasts and other moving things come to you in the cave. I did not let the serpent come with them because it might have risen against you and made you tremble; and the fear of it should fall into your hearts.

5 For I knew that the accursed one is wicked; therefore I would not let it come near you with the other beasts.

6 But now strengthen your heart and fear not. I am with you to the end of the days I have determined on you."

Chapter XX - Adam wishes to protect Eve.

1 Then Adam cried and said, "O God, take us away to some other place, where the serpent can not come near us again, and rise against us. For fear that it might find Your handmaid Eve alone and kill her; for its eyes are hideous and evil."

2 But God said to Adam and Eve, "From now on, don't be afraid, I will not let it come near you; I have driven it away from you, from this mountain; neither will I leave in it the ability to hurt you."

3 Then Adam and Eve worshipped before God and gave Him thanks, and praised Him for having delivered them from death.

Chapter XXI - Adam and Eve attempt suicide.

1 Then Adam and Eve went in search of the garden.

2 And the heat beat like a flame on their faces; and they sweated from the heat, and cried before the Lord.

3 But the place where they cried was close to a high mountain, facing the western gate of the garden.

4 Then Adam threw himself down from the top of that mountain; his face was torn and his flesh was ripped; he lost a lot of blood and was close to death.

5 Meanwhile Eve remained standing on the mountain crying over him, thus lying.

6 And she said, "I don't wish to live after him; for all that he did to himself was through me."

7 Then she threw herself after him; and was torn and ripped by stones; and remained lying as dead.

8 But the merciful God, who looks over His creatures, looked at Adam and Eve as they lay dead, and He sent His Word to them, and raised them.

9 And said to Adam, "O Adam, all this misery which you have brought on yourself, will have no affect against My rule, neither will it alter the covenant of the 5, 500 years."

Chapter XXII - Adam in a gracious mood.

1 Then Adam said to God, "I dry up in the heat, I am faint from walking, and I don't want to be in this world. And I don't know when You will take me out of it to rest."

2 Then the Lord God said to him, "O Adam, it cannot be now, not until you have ended your days. Then shall I bring you out of this miserable land."

3 And Adam said to God, "While I was in the garden I knew neither heat, nor languor, neither moving about, nor trembling, nor fear; but now since I came to this land, all this affliction has come over me.

4 Then God said to Adam, "So long as you were keeping My commandment, My light and My grace rested on you. But when you transgressed My commandment, sorrow and misery came to you in this land."

5 And Adam cried and said, "O Lord, do not cut me off for this, neither punish me with heavy plagues, nor yet repay me according to my sin; for we, of our own will, transgressed Your commandment, and ignored Your law, and tried to become gods like you, when Satan the enemy deceived us."

6 Then God said again to Adam, "Because you have endured fear and trembling in this land, languor and suffering, treading and walking about, going on this mountain, and dying from it, I will take all this on Myself in order to save you."

Chapter XXIII - Adam and Eve strengthen themselves and make the first altar ever built.

1 Then Adam cried more and said, "O God, have mercy on me, so far as to take on yourself, that which I will do."

2 But God withdrew His Word from Adam and Eve.

3 Then Adam and Eve stood on their feet; and Adam said to Eve, "Strengthen yourself, and I also will strengthen myself." And she strengthened herself, as Adam told her.

4 Then Adam and Eve took stones and placed them in the shape of an altar; and they took leaves from the trees outside the garden, with which they wiped, from the face of the rock, the blood they had spilled.

5 But that which had dropped on the sand, they took together with the dust with which it was mingled and offered it on the altar as an offering to God.

6 Then Adam and Eve stood under the Altar and cried, thus praying to God, "Forgive us our trespass* and our sin, and look at us with Thine eye of mercy. For when we were in the garden our praises and our hymns went up before you without ceasing.

7 But when we came into this strange land, pure praise was not longer ours, nor righteous prayer, nor understanding hearts, nor sweet thoughts, nor just counsels, nor long discernment, nor upright feelings, neither is our bright nature left us. But our body is changed from the likeness in which it was at first, when we were created.

8 Yet now look at our blood which is offered on these stones, and accept it at our hands, like the praise we used to sing to you at first, when in the garden."

9 And Adam began to make more requests of God.

* ORIGINAL OF THE LORD'S PRAYER SAID TO BE USED ABOUT 150 YEARS BEFORE OUR LORD: Our Father, Who art in Heaven, be gracious unto us, O Lord our God, hallowed be Your Name, and let the remembrance of Thee be glorified Heaven above and upon earth here below.

Let Your kingdom reign over us now and forever. The Holy Men of old said remit and forgive unto all men whatsoever they have done unto me. And lead us not into temptation, but deliver us from the evil thing; for Thine is the kingdom and Thou shalt reign in glory forever and forevermore, AMEN.

Chapter XXIV - A vivid prophecy of the life and death of Christ.

1 Then the merciful God, good and lover of men, looked at Adam and Eve, and at their blood, which they had held up as an offering to Him; without an order from Him for so doing. But He wondered at them; and accepted their offerings.

2 And God sent from His presence a bright fire, that consumed their offering.

3 He smelled the sweet savor of their offering, and showed them mercy.

4 Then came the Word of God to Adam, and said to him, "O Adam, as you have shed your blood, so will I shed My own blood when I become flesh of your descendants; and as you died, O Adam, so also will I die. And as you built an altar, so also will I make for you an altar of the earth; and as you offered your blood on it, so also will I offer My blood on an altar on the earth.

5 And as you sued for forgiveness through that blood, so also will I make My blood forgiveness of sins, and erase transgressions in it.

6 And now, behold, I have accepted your offering, O Adam, but the days of the covenant in which I have bound you are not fulfilled. When they are fulfilled, then will I bring you back into the garden.

7 Now, therefore, strengthen your heart; and when sorrow comes over you, make Me an offering, and I will be favorable to you."

Chapter XXV - God represented as merciful and loving. The establishing of worship.

1 But God knew that Adam believed he should frequently kill himself and make an offering to Him of his blood.

2 Therefore He said to him, "O Adam, don't ever kill yourself like this again, by throwing yourself down from that mountain."

3 But Adam said to God, "I was thinking to put an end to myself at once, for having transgressed Your commandments, and for my having come out of the beautiful garden; and for the bright light of which You have deprived me; and for the praises which poured forth from my mouth without ceasing, and for the light that covered me.

4 Yet of Your goodness, O God, do not get rid of me altogether; but be favorable to me every time I die, and bring me to life.

5 And thereby it will be made known that You are a merciful God, who does not want anyone to perish; who loves not that one should fall; and who does not condemn any one cruelly, badly, and by whole destruction."

6 Then Adam remained silent.

7 And the Word of God came to him, and blessed him, and comforted him, and covenanted with him, that He would save him at the end of the days determined for him.

8 This, then, was the first offering Adam made to God; and so it became his custom to do.

Chapter XXVI - A beautiful prophecy of eternal life and joy (v. 15). The fall of night.

1 Then Adam took Eve, and they began to return to the Cave of Treasures where they lived. But when they got closer to it and saw it from a distance, heavy sorrow fell on Adam and Eve when they looked at it.

2 Then Adam said to Eve, "When we were on the mountain we were comforted by the Word of God that conversed with us; and the light that came from the east shown over us.

3 But now the Word of God is hidden from us; and the light that shown over us is so changed as to disappear, and let darkness and sorrow come over us.

4 And we are forced to enter this cave which is like a prison, in which darkness covers us, so that we are separated from each other; and you can not see me, neither can I see you."

5 When Adam had said these words, they cried and spread their hands before God; for they were full of sorrow.

6 And they prayed to God to bring the sun to them, to shine on them, so that darkness would not return to them, and that they wouldn't have to go under this covering of rock. And they wished to die rather than see the darkness.

7 Then God looked at Adam and Eve and at their great sorrow, and at all they had done with a fervent heart, on account of all the trouble they were in, instead of their former well-being, and on account of all the misery that came over them in a strange land.

8 Therefore God was not angry with them; nor impatient with them; but he was patient and forbearing towards them, as towards the children He had created.

9 Then came the Word of God to Adam, and said to him, "Adam, as for the sun, if I were to take it and bring it to you, days, hours, years and months would all stop, and the covenant I have made with you, would never be fulfilled.

10 But then you would be deserted and stuck in a perpetual plague, and you would never be saved.

11 Yes, rather, bear long and calm your soul while you live night and day; until the fulfillment of the days, and the time of My covenant is come.

12 Then shall I come and save you, O Adam, for I do not wish that you be afflicted.

13 And when I look at all the good things in which you lived, and why you came out of them, then would I willingly show you mercy.

14 But I cannot alter the covenant that has gone out of My mouth; otherwise I would have brought you back into the garden.

15 When, however, the covenant is fulfilled, then shall I show you and your descendants mercy, and bring you into a land of gladness, where there is neither sorrow nor suffering; but abiding joy and gladness, and light that never fails, and praises that never cease; and a beautiful garden that shall never pass away."

16 And God said again to Adam, "Be patient and enter the cave, for the darkness, of which you were afraid, shall only be twelve hours long; and when ended, light shall come up."

17 Then when Adam heard these words from God, he and Eve worshipped before Him, and their hearts were comforted. They returned into the cave after their custom, while tears flowed from their eyes, sorrow and wailing came from their hearts, and they wished their soul would leave their body.

18 And Adam and Eve stood praying until the darkness of night came over them, and Adam was hid from Eve, and she from him.

19 And they remained standing in prayer.

Chapter XXVII - The second tempting of Adam and Eve. The devil takes on the form of a beguiling light.

1 When Satan, the hater of all good, saw how they continued in prayer, and how God communed with them, and comforted them, and how He had accepted their offering—Satan made an apparition.

2 He began with transforming his hosts; in his hands was a flashing fire, and they were in a great light.

3 He then placed his throne near the mouth of the cave because he could not enter into it by reason of their prayers. And he shed light into the cave, until the cave glistened over Adam and Eve; while his hosts began to sing praises.

4 And Satan did this, in order that when Adam saw the light, he should think within himself that it was a heavenly light, and that Satan's hosts were angels; and that God had sent them to watch at the cave, and to give him light in the darkness.

5 So that when Adam came out of the cave and saw them, and Adam and Eve bowed to Satan, then he would overcome Adam thereby, and a second time humble him before God.

6 When, therefore, Adam and Eve saw the light, fancying it was real, they strengthened their hearts; yet, as they were trembling, Adam said to Eve:—

7 "Look at that great light, and at those many songs of praise, and at that host standing outside who won't come into our cave. Why don't they tell us what they want, where they are from, what the meaning of this light is, what those praises are, why they have been sent to this place, and why they won't come in?

8 If they were from God, they would come into the cave with us, and would tell us why they were sent."

9 Then Adam stood up and prayed to God with a burning heart, and said:—

10 "O Lord, is there in the world another god besides You, who created angels and filled them with light, and sent them to keep us, who would come with them?

11 But, look, we see these hosts that stand at the mouth of the cave; they are in a great light; they sing loud praises. If they are of some other god than You, tell me; and if they are sent by you, inform me of the reason for which You have sent them."

12 No sooner had Adam said this, than an angel from God appeared to him in the cave, who said to him, "O Adam, fear not. This is Satan and his hosts; he wishes to deceive you as he deceived you at first. For the first time, he was hidden in the serpent; but this time he is come to you in the likeness of an angel of light; in order that, when you worshipped him, he might enslave you, in the very presence of God."

13 Then the angel went from Adam and seized Satan at the opening of the cave, and stripped him of the pretense he had assumed, and brought him in his own hideous form to Adam and Eve; who were afraid of him when they saw him.

14 And the angel said to Adam, "This hideous form has been his ever since God made him fall from heaven. He could not have come near you in it; he therefore transformed himself into an angel of light."

15 Then the angel drove away Satan and his hosts from Adam and Eve, and said to them, "Fear not; God who created you, will strengthen you."

16 And the angel left them.

17 But Adam and Eve remained standing in the cave; no consolation came to them; they divided in their thoughts.

18 And when it was morning they prayed; and then went out to seek the garden. For their hearts were towards it, and they could get no consolation for having left it.

Chapter XXVIII - The Devil pretends to lead Adam and Eve to the water to bathe.

1 But when the crafty Satan saw them, that they were going to the garden, he gathered together his host, and came in appearance on a cloud, intent on deceiving them.

2 But when Adam and Eve saw him thus in a vision, they thought they were angels of God come to comfort them about having left the garden, or to bring them back again into it.

3 And Adam spread his hands before God, beseeching Him to make him understand what they were.

4 Then Satan, the hater of all good, said to Adam, "O Adam, I am an angel of the great God; and, behold the hosts that surround me.

5 God has sent us to take you and bring you to the border of the garden northwards; to the shore of the clear sea, and bathe you and Eve in it, and raise you to your former gladness, that you return again to the garden."

6 These words sank into the heart of Adam and Eve.

7 Yet God withheld His Word from Adam, and did not make him understand at once, but waited to see his strength; whether he would be overcome as Eve was when in the garden, or whether he would prevail.

8 Then Satan called to Adam and Eve, and said, "Behold, we go to the sea of water," and they began to go.

9 And Adam and Eve followed them at some little distance.

10 But when they came to the mountain to the north of the garden, a very high mountain, without any steps to the top of it, the Devil drew near to Adam and Eve, and made them go up to the top in reality, and not in a vision; wishing, as he did, to throw them down and kill

them, and to wipe off their name from the earth; so that this earth should remain to him and his hosts alone.

Chapter XXIX - God tells Adam of the Devil's purpose. (v. 4).

1 But when the merciful God saw that Satan wished to kill Adam with his many tricks, and saw that Adam was meek and without guile, God spoke to Satan in a loud voice, and cursed him.

2 Then he and his hosts fled, and Adam and Eve remained standing on the top of the mountain, from there they saw below them the wide world, high above which they were. But they saw none of the host which time after time were by them.

3 They cried, both Adam and Eve, before God, and begged for forgiveness of Him.

4 Then came the Word from God to Adam, and said to him, "Know you and understand concerning this Satan, that he seeks to deceive you and your descendants after you."

5 And Adam cried before the Lord God, and begged and prayed to Him to give him something from the garden, as a token to him, wherein to be comforted.

6 And God considered Adam's thought, and sent the angel Michael as far as the sea that reaches India, to take from there golden rods and bring them to Adam.

7 This did God in His wisdom in order that these golden rods, being with Adam in the cave, should shine forth with light in the night around him, and put an end to his fear of the darkness.

8 Then the angel Michael went down by God's order, took golden rods, as God had commanded him, and brought them to God.

Chapter XXX - Adam receives the first worldly goods.

1 After these things, God commanded the angel Gabriel to go down to the garden, and say to the cherub who kept it, "Behold, God has commanded me to come into the garden, and to take from it sweet smelling incense, and give it to Adam."

2 Then the angel Gabriel went down by God's order to the garden, and told the cherub as God had commanded him.

3 The cherub then said, "Well." And Gabriel went in and took the incense.

4 Then God commanded his angel Raphael to go down to the garden, and speak to the cherub about some myrrh, to give to Adam.

5 And the angel Raphael went down and told the cherub as God had commanded him, and the cherub said, "Well." Then Raphael went in and took the myrrh.

6 The golden rods were from the Indian sea, where there are precious stones. The incense was from the eastern border of the garden; and the myrrh from the western border, from where bitterness came over Adam.

7 And the angels brought these things to God, by the Tree of Life, in the garden.

8 Then God said to the angels, "Dip them in the spring of water; then take them and sprinkle their water over Adam and Eve, that they be a little comforted in their sorrow, and give them to Adam and Eve.

9 And the angels did as God had commanded them, and they gave all those things to Adam and Eve on the top of the mountain on which Satan had placed them, when he sought to make an end of them.

10 And when Adam saw the golden rods, the incense and the myrrh, he was rejoiced and cried because he thought that the gold was a token of the kingdom from where he had come, that the incense was a token of the bright light which had been taken from him, and that the myrrh was a token of the sorrow in which he was.

Chapter XXXI - They make themselves more comfortable in the Cave of Treasures on the third day.

1 After these things God said to Adam, "You asked Me for something from the garden, to be comforted therewith, and I have given you these three tokens as a consolation to you; that you trust in Me and in My covenant with you.

2 For I will come and save you; and kings shall bring me when in the flesh, gold, incense and myrrh; gold as a token of My kingdom; incense as a token of My divinity; and myrrh as a token of My suffering and of My death.

3 But, O Adam, put these by you in the cave; the gold that it may shed light over you by night; the incense, that you smell its sweet savor; and the myrrh, to comfort you in your sorrow."

4 When Adam heard these words from God, he worshipped before Him. He and Eve worshipped Him and gave Him thanks, because He had dealt mercifully with them.

5 Then God commanded the three angels, Michael, Gabriel and Raphael, each to bring what he had brought, and give it to Adam. And they did so, one by one.

6 And God commanded Suriyel and Salathiel to bear up Adam and Eve, and bring them down from the top of the high mountain, and to take them to the Cave of Treasures.

7 There they laid the gold on the south side of the cave, the incense on the eastern side, and the myrrh on the western side. For the mouth of the cave was on the north side.

8 The angels then comforted Adam and Eve, and departed.

9 The gold was seventy rods*; the incense, twelve pounds; and the myrrh, three pounds.

10 These remained by Adam in the Cave of Treasures**.

11 God gave these three things to Adam on the third day after he had come out of the garden, in token of the three days the Lord should remain in the heart of the earth.

12 And these three things, as they continued with Adam in the cave, gave him light by night; and by day they gave him a little relief from his sorrow.

* A rod is a unit of linear measure equivalent to 5.5 yards and also a unit of area measure equivalent to 30.25 square yards. In this case, the word rod simply means a kind of long, thin piece of gold of unspecified size and weight.

** This is the original text which appears to contain embedded editorial content: "These remained by Adam in the House of Treasures; therefore was it called 'of concealment.' But other interpreters say it was called the 'Cave of Treasures,' by reason of the bodies of righteous men that were in it.

Chapter XXXII - Adam and Eve go into the water to pray.

1 And Adam and Eve remained in the Cave of Treasures until the seventh day; they neither ate of the fruit the earth, nor drank water.

2 And when it dawned on the eighth day, Adam said to Eve, "O Eve, we prayed God to give us something from the garden, and He sent his angels who brought us what we had desired.

3 But now, get up, let us go to the sea of water we saw at first, and let us stand in it, praying that God will again be favorable to us and take us back to the garden; or give us something; or that He will give us comfort in some other land than this in which we are."

4 Then Adam and Eve came out of the cave, went and stood on the border of the sea in which they had before thrown themselves, and Adam said to Eve:—

5 Come, go down into this place, and come not out of it until the end of thirty days, when I shall come to you. And pray to God with burning heart and a sweet voice, to forgive us.

6 And I will go to another place, and go down into it, and do like you."

7 Then Eve went down into the water, as Adam had commanded her. Adam also went down into the water; and they stood praying; and besought the Lord to forgive them their offense, and to restore them to their former state.

8 And they stood like that praying, until the end of the thirty-five days.

Chapter XXXIII - Satan falsely promises the "bright light."

1 But Satan, the hater of all good, sought them in the cave, but found them not, although he searched diligently for them.

2 But he found them standing in the water praying and thought within himself, "Adam and Eve are standing like that in that water praying to God to forgive them their transgression, and to restore them to their former state, and to take them from under my hand.

3 But I will deceive them so that they shall come out of the water, and not fulfil their vow."

4 Then the hater of all good, went not to Adam, but he went to Eve, and took the form of an angel of God, praising and rejoicing, and said to her:—

5 "Peace be to you! Be glad and rejoice! God is favorable to you, and He sent me to Adam. I have brought him the glad tidings of salvation, and of his being filled with bright light as he was at first.

6 And Adam, in his joy for his restoration, has sent me to you, that you come to me, in order that I crown you with light like him.

7 And he said to me, 'Speak to Eve; if she does not come with you, tell her of the sign when we were on the top of the mountain; how God sent his angels who took us and brought us to the Cave of Treasures; and laid the gold on the southern side; incense, on the eastern side; and myrrh on the western side.' Now come to him."

8 When Eve hear these words from him, she rejoiced greatly. And thinking Satan's appearance was real, she came out of the sea.

9 He went before, and she followed him until they came to Adam. Then Satan hid himself from her, and she saw him no more.

10 She then came and stood before Adam, who was standing by the water and rejoicing in God's forgiveness.

11 And as she called to him, he turned around, found her there and cried when he saw her, and beat his chest; and from the bitterness of his grief, he sank into the water.

12 But God looked at him and at his misery, and at his being about to breathe his last. And the Word of God came from heaven, raised him out of the water, and said to him, "Go up the high bank to Eve." And when he came up to Eve he said to her, "Who told you to come here?"

13 Then she told him the discourse of the angel who had appeared to her and had given her a sign.

14 But Adam grieved, and gave her to know it was Satan. He then took her and they both returned to the cave.

15 These things happened to them the second time they went down to the water, seven days after their coming out of the garden.

16 They fasted in the water thirty-five days; altogether forty-two days since they had left the garden.

Chapter XXXIV - Adam recalls the creation of Eve. He eloquently appeals for food and drink.

1 And on the morning of the forty-third day, they came out of the cave, sorrowful and crying. Their bodies were lean, and they were parched from hunger and thirst, from fasting and praying, and from their heavy sorrow on account of their transgression.

2 And when they had come out of the cave they went up the mountain to the west of the garden.

3 There they stood and prayed and besought God to grant them forgiveness of their sins.

4 And after their prayers Adam began to beg God, saying, "O my Lord, my God, and my Creator, You commanded the four elements* to be gathered together, and they were gathered together by Thine order.

5 Then You spread Your hand and created me out of one element, that of dust of the earth; and You brought me into the garden at the third hour, on a Friday, and informed me of it in the cave.

6 Then, at first, I knew neither night nor day, for I had a bright nature; neither did the light in which I lived ever leave me to know night or day.

7 Then, again, O Lord, in that third hour in which You created me, You brought to me all beasts, and lions, and ostriches, and fowls of the air, and all things that move in the earth, which You had created at the first hour before me of the Friday.

8 And Your will was that I should name them all, one by one, with a suitable name. But You gave me understanding and knowledge, and a pure heart and a right mind from you, that I should name them after Thine own mind regarding the naming of them.

9 O God, You made them obedient to me, and ordered that not one of them break from my sway, according to Your commandment, and to the dominion which You had given me over them. But now they are all estranged from me.

10 Then it was in that third hour of Friday, in which You created me, and commanded me concerning the tree, to which I was neither to go near, nor to eat thereof; for You said to me in the garden, 'When you eat of it, of death you shall die.'

11 And if You had punished me as You said, with death, I should have died that very moment.

12 Moreover, when You commanded me regarding the tree, I was neither to approach nor to eat thereof, Eve was not with me; You had not yet created her, neither had You yet taken her out of my side; nor had she yet heard this order from you.

13 Then, at the end of the third hour of that Friday, O Lord, You caused a slumber and a sleep to come over me, and I slept, and was overwhelmed in sleep.

14 Then You drew a rib out of my side, and created it after my own likeness and image. Then I awoke; and when I saw her and knew who she was, I said, 'This is bone of my bones, and flesh of my flesh; from now on she shall be called woman.'

15 It was of Your good will, O God, that You brought a slumber in a sleep over me, and that You immediately brought Eve out of my side, until she was out, so that I did not see how she was made; neither could I witness, O my Lord, how awful and great are Your goodness and glory.

16 And of Your goodwill, O Lord, You made us both with bodies of a bright nature, and You made us two, one; and You gave us Your grace, and filled us with praises of the Holy Spirit; that we should be neither hungry nor thirsty, nor know what sorrow is, nor yet faintness of heart; neither suffering, fasting nor weariness.

17 But now, O God, since we transgressed Your commandment and broke Your law, You have brought us out into a strange land, and have caused suffering, and faintness, hunger and thirst to come over us.

18 Now, therefore, O God, we pray you, give us something to eat from the garden, to satisfy our hunger with it; and something wherewith to quench our thirst.

19 For, behold, many days, O God, we have tasted nothing and drunk nothing, and our flesh is dried up, and our strength is wasted, and sleep is gone from our eyes from faintness and crying.

20 Then, O God, we dare not gather anything from the fruit of trees, from fear of you. For when we transgress at first You spared us and did not make us die.

21 But now, we thought in our hearts, if we eat of the fruit of the trees, without God's order, He will destroy us this time, and will wipe us off from the face of the earth.

22 And if we drink of this water, without God's order, He will make an end of us and root us up at once.

23 Now, therefore, O God, that I am come to this place with Eve, we beg You to give us some fruit from the garden, that we may be satisfied with it.

24 For we desire the fruit that is on the earth, and all else that we lack in it."

* The medieval belief that there were only four elements—fire, earth, air, and water—was widely accepted until about 1500 AD when the current atomic theory was in its infancy.

Chapter XXXV - God's reply.

1 Then God looked again at Adam and his crying and groaning, and the Word of God came to him, and said to him:—

2 "O Adam, when you were in My garden, you knew neither eating nor drinking; neither faintness nor suffering; neither leanness of flesh, nor change; neither did sleep depart from thine eyes. But since you transgressed, and came into this strange land, all these trials are come over you."

Chapter XXXVI - Figs.

1 Then God commanded the cherub, who kept the gate of the garden with a sword of fire in his hand, to take some of the fruit of the fig-tree, and to give it to Adam.

2 The cherub obeyed the command of the Lord God, and went into the garden and brought two figs on two twigs, each fig hanging to its leaf; they were from two of the trees among which Adam and Eve hid themselves when God went to walk in the garden, and the Word of God came to Adam and Eve and said to them, "Adam, Adam, where are you?"

3 And Adam answered, "O God, here I am. When I heard the sound of You and Your voice, I hid myself, because I am naked."

4 Then the cherub took two figs and brought them to Adam and Eve. But he threw them to them from a distance; for they might not come near the cherub by reason of their flesh, that could not come near the fire.

5 At first, angels trembled at the presence of Adam and were afraid of him. But now Adam trembled before the angels and was afraid of them.

6 Then Adam came closer and took one fig, and Eve also came in turn and took the other.

7 And as they took them up in their hands, they looked at them, and knew they were from the trees among which they had hidden themselves.

Chapter XXXVII - Forty-three days of penance do not redeem one hour of sin (v. 6).

1 Then Adam said to Eve, "Do you not see these figs and their leaves, with which we covered ourselves when we were stripped of our bright nature? But now, we do not know what misery and suffering may come over us from eating them.

2 Now, therefore, O Eve, let us restrain ourselves and not eat of them, you and I; and let us ask God to give us of the fruit of the Tree of Life."

3 Thus did Adam and Eve restrain themselves, and did not eat of these figs.

4 But Adam began to pray to God and to beseech Him to give him of the fruit of the Tree of Life, saying thus: "O God, when we transgressed Your commandment at the sixth hour of Friday, we were stripped of the bright nature we had, and did not continue in the garden after our transgression, more than three hours.

5 But in the evening You made us come out of it. O God, we transgressed against You one hour, and all these trials and sorrows have come over us until this day.

6 And those days together with this the forty-third day, do not redeem that one hour in which we transgressed!

7 O God, look at us with an eye of pity, and do not avenge us according to our transgression of Your commandment, in Your presence.

8 O God, give us of the fruit of the Tree of Life, that we may eat of it, and live, and turn not to see sufferings and other trouble, in this earth; for You are God.

9 When we transgressed Your commandment, You made us come out of the garden, and sent a cherub to keep the Tree of Life, lest we should eat thereof, and live; and know nothing of faintness after we transgressed.

10 But now, O Lord, behold, we have endured all these days, and have borne sufferings. Make these forty-three days an equivalent for the one hour in which we transgressed."

Chapter XXXVIII - "When 5500 years are fulfilled...."

1 After these things the Word of God came to Adam, and said to him:—

2 "O Adam, as to the fruit on the Tree of Life that you have asked for, I will not give it to you now, but only when the 5500 years are fulfilled. At that time I will give you fruit from the Tree of Life, and you will eat, and live forever, you, and Eve, and your righteous descendants.

3 But these forty-three days cannot make amends for the hour in which you transgressed My commandment.

4 O Adam, I gave you the fruit of the fig-tree to eat in which you hid yourself. Go and eat of it, you and Eve.

5 I will not deny your request, neither will I disappoint your hope; therefore, endure until the fulfillment of the covenant I made with you."

6 And God withdrew His Word from Adam.

Chapter XXXIX - Adam is cautious—but too late.

1 Then Adam returned to Eve, and said to her, "Get up, and take a fig for yourself, and I will take another; and let us go to our cave."

2 Then Adam and Eve took each a fig and went towards the cave; the time was about the setting of the sun; and their thoughts made them long to eat of the fruit.

3 But Adam said to Eve, "I am afraid to eat of this fig. I know not what may come over me from it."

4 So Adam cried, and stood praying before God, saying, "Satisfy my hunger, without my having to eat this fig; for after I have eaten it, what will it profit me? And what shall I desire and ask of you, O God, when it is gone?"

5 And he said again, "I am afraid to eat of it; for I know not what will befall me through it."

Chapter XL - The first Human hunger.

1 Then the Word of God came to Adam, and said to him, "O Adam, why didn't you have this dread, or this fasting, or this care before now? And why didn't you have this fear before you transgressed?

2 But when you came to live in this strange land, your animal body could not survive on earth without earthly food, to strengthen it and to restore its powers."

3 And God withdrew His Word for Adam.

Chapter XLI - The first Human thirst.

1 Then Adam took the fig, and laid it on the golden rods. Eve also took her fig, and put it on the incense.

2 And the weight of each fig was that of a water-melon; for the fruit of the garden was much larger than the fruit of this land*.

3 But Adam and Eve remained standing and fasting the whole of that night, until the morning dawned.

4 When the sun rose they were still praying, but after they had finished praying, Adam said to Eve:—

5 "O Eve, come, let us go to the border of the garden looking south; to the place from where the river flows, and is parted into four heads. There we will pray to God, and ask Him to give us some of the Water of Life to drink.

6 For God has not fed us with the Tree of Life, in order that we may not live. Therefore, we will ask him to give us some of the Water of Life, and to quench our thirst with it, rather than with a drink of water of this land."

7 When Eve heard these words from Adam, she agreed; and they both got up and came to the southern border of the garden, at the edge of the river of water a short distance from the garden.

8 And they stood and prayed before the Lord, and asked Him to look at them this once, to forgive them, and to grant them their request.

9 After this prayer from both of them, Adam began to pray with his voice before God, and said;—

10 "O Lord, when I was in the garden and saw the water that flowed from under the Tree of Life, my heart did not desire, neither did my body require to drink of it; neither did I know thirst, for I was living; and above that which I am now.

11 So that in order to live I did not require any Food of Life, neither did I drink of the Water of Life.

12 But now, O God, I am dead; my flesh is parched with thirst. Give me of the Water of Life that I may drink of it and live.

13 Of Your mercy, O God, save me from these plagues and trials, and bring me into another land different from this, if You will not let me live in Your garden."

* This is substantiated by Genesis 3:7 whereby the leaves of the fig tree were large enough that Adam and Eve could fashion garments from them.

Chapter XLII - A promise of the Water of Life. The third prophecy of the coming of Christ.

1 Then came the Word of God to Adam, and said to him:—

31

2 "O Adam, as to what you said, 'Bring me into a land where there is rest,' it is not another land than this, but it is the kingdom of heaven where alone there is rest.

3 But you can not make your entrance into it at present; but only after your judgment is past and fulfilled.

4 Then will I make you go up into the kingdom of heaven, you and your righteous descendants; and I will give you and them the rest you ask for at present.

5 And if you said, 'Give me of the Water of Life that I may drink and live'—it cannot be this day, but on the day that I shall descend into hell, and break the gates of brass, and bruise in pieces the kingdoms of iron.

6 Then will I in mercy save your soul and the souls of the righteous, to give them rest in My garden. And that shall be when the end of the world is come.

7 And, again, in regards to the Water of Life you seek, it will not be granted you this day; but on the day that I shall shed My blood on your head* in the land of Golgotha**.

8 For My blood shall be the Water of Life to you at that time, and not to just you alone, but to all your descendants who shall believe in Me***; that it be to them for rest forever."

9 The Lord said again to Adam, "O Adam, when you were in the garden, these trials did not come to you.

10 But since you transgressed My commandment, all these sufferings have come over you.

11 Now, also, does your flesh require food and drink; drink then of that water that flows by you on the face of the earth.

12 Then God withdrew His Word from Adam.

13 And Adam and Eve worshipped the Lord, and returned from the river of water to the cave. It was noon-day; and when they drew near to the cave, they saw a large fire by it.

* This phrase indicates that the bleeding will take place in an elevated position above the populace. This is believed to be a reference to the cross whereby Christ bled profusely above the people below.

** Golgotha (goal-goth-uh) was the hill outside the walls of Jerusalem where Jesus was crucified. Its exact location is not precisely known, but the Church of the Holy Sepulcher is believed to have been constructed on this hill.

*** Reference: John 6:25 and 7:38

1 Then Adam and Eve were afraid, and stood still. And Adam said to Eve, "What is that fire by our cave? We have done nothing in it to cause this fire.

2 We neither have bread to bake therein, nor broth to cook there. As to this fire, we have never known anything like it, neither do we know what to call it.

3 But ever since God sent the cherub with a sword of fire that flashed and lightened in his hand, from fear of which we fell down and were like corpses, have we not seen the like.

4 But now, O Eve, behold, this is the same fire that was in the cherub's hand, which God has sent to keep the cave in which we live.

5 O Eve, it is because God is angry with us, and will drive us from it.

6 O Eve, we have again transgressed His commandment in that cave, so that He had sent this fire to burn around it, and to prevent us from going into it.

7 If this be really so, O Eve, where shall we live? And where shall we flee from before the face of the Lord? Since, in regards to the garden, He will not let us live in it, and He has deprived us of the good things thereof; but He has placed us in this cave, in which we have borne darkness, trials and hardships, until at last we have found comfort therein.

8 But now that He has brought us out into another land, who knows what may happen in it? And who knows but that the darkness of that land may be far greater than the darkness of this land?

9 Who knows what may happen in that land by day or by night? And who knows whether it will be far or near, O Eve? Where it will please God to put us, may be far from the garden, O Eve? Or where God will prevent us from beholding Him, because we have transgressed His commandment, and because we have made requests of Him at all times?

10 O Eve, if God will bring us into a strange land other than this, in which we find consolation, it must be to put our souls to death, and blot out our name from the face of the earth.

11 O Eve, if we are further alienated from the garden and from God, where shall we find Him again, and ask Him to give us gold, incense, myrrh, and some fruit of the fig-tree?

12 Where shall we find Him, to comfort us a second time? Where shall we find Him, that He may think of us, as regards the covenant He has made on our behalf?"

13 Then Adam said no more. And they kept looking, He and Eve, towards the cave, and at the fire that flared up around it.

14 But that fire was from Satan. For he had gathered trees and dry grasses, and had carried and brought them to the cave, and had set fire to them, in order to consume the cave and what was in it.

15 So that Adam and Eve should be left in sorrow, and he should cut off their trust in God, and make them deny Him.

16 But by the mercy of God he could not burn the cave, for God sent His angel around the cave to guard it from such a fire, until it went out.

17 And this fire lasted from noon-day until the break of day. That was the forty-fifth day.

Chapter XLIV - The power of fire over man.

1 Yet Adam and Eve were standing and looking at the fire, and unable to come near the cave from their dread of the fire.

2 And Satan kept on bringing trees and throwing them into the fire, until the flames of the fire rose up on high, and covered the whole cave, thinking, as he did in his own mind, to consume the cave with much fire. But the angel of the Lord was guarding it.

3 And yet he could not curse Satan, nor injure him by word, because he had no authority over him, neither did he take to doing so with words from his mouth.

4 Therefore the angel tolerated him, without saying one bad word, until the Word of God came who said to Satan, "Go away from here; once before you deceived My servants, and this time you seek to destroy them.

5 Were it not for My mercy I would have destroyed you and your hosts from off the earth. But I have had patience with you, until the end of the world."

6 Then Satan fled from before the Lord. But the fire went on burning around the cave like a coal-fire the whole day; which was the forty-sixth day Adam and Eve had spent since they came out of the garden.

7 And when Adam and Eve saw that the heat of the fire had somewhat cooled down, they began to walk towards the cave to get into it as they usually did; but they could not, by reason of the heat of the fire.

8 Then they both began crying because of the fire that separated them from the cave, and that came towards them, burning. And they were afraid.

9 Then Adam said to Eve, "See this fire of which we have a portion in us: which formerly yielded to us, but no longer does so, now that we have transgressed the limit of creation, and changed our condition, and our nature is altered. But the fire is not changed in its nature, nor altered from its creation. Therefore it now has power over us; and when we come near it, it scorches our flesh."

Chapter XLV - Why Satan didn't fulfil his promises. Description of hell.

1 Then Adam rose and prayed to God, saying, "See, this fire has separated us from the cave in which You have commanded us to live; but now, behold, we cannot go into it."

2 Then God heard Adam, and sent him His Word, that said:—

3 "O Adam, see this fire! How different the flame and heat thereof are from the garden of delights and the good things in it!

4 When you were under My control, all creatures yielded to you; but after you have transgressed My commandment, they all rise over you."

5 God said again to him, "See, O Adam, how Satan has exalted you! He has deprived you of the Godhead, and of an exalted state like Me, and has not kept his word to you; but has, after all, become your enemy. He is the one who made this fire in which he meant to burn you and Eve.

6 Why, O Adam, has he not kept his agreement with you, not even one day; but has deprived you of the glory that was on you—when you yielded to his command?

7 Do you think, Adam, that he loved you when he made this agreement with you? Or that he loved you and wished to raise you on high?

8 But no, Adam, he did not do all that out of love to you; but he wished to make you come out of light into darkness; and from an exalted state to degradation; from glory to abasement; from joy to sorrow; and from rest to fasting and fainting."

9 God also said to Adam, "See this fire kindled by Satan around your cave; see this wonder that surrounds you; and know that it will encompass about both you and your descendants, when you obey his command; that he will plague you with fire; and that you will go down into hell after you are dead.

10 Then you will see the burning of his fire, that will be burning around you and likewise your descendants. You will not be delivered from it until My coming; just like you cannot go into your cave right now because of the great fire around it; not until My Word comes and makes a way for you on the day My covenant is fulfilled.

11 There is no way for you at present to come from this life to rest, not until My Word comes, who is My Word. Then He will make a way for you, and you shall have rest." Then God called with His Word to the fire that burned around the cave, that it split itself in half, until Adam had gone through it. Then the fire parted itself by God's order, and a way was made for Adam*.

12 And God withdrew His Word from Adam.

* Reference: Exodus 14:21,22 and Joshua 3:15-17

Chapter XLVI - "How many times have I delivered you out of his hand . . ."

1 Then Adam and Eve began again to come into the cave. And when they came to the way between the fire, Satan blew into the fire like a whirlwind, and caused the burning coal-fire to cover Adam and Eve; so that their bodies were singed; and the coal-fire scorched them*.

2 And from the burning of the fire Adam and Eve screamed, and said, "O Lord, save us! Leave us not to be consumed and plagued by this burning fire; neither require us for having transgressed Your commandment."

3 Then God looked at their bodies, on which Satan had caused fire to burn, and God sent His angel that stayed the burning fire. But the wounds remained on their bodies.

4 And God said to Adam, "See Satan's love for you, who pretended to give you the Godhead and greatness; and, behold, he burns you with fire, and seeks to destroy you from off the earth.

5 Then look at Me, O Adam; I created you, and how many times have I delivered you out of his hand? If not, wouldn't he have destroyed you?"

6 God said again to Eve, "What is that he promised you in the garden, saying, 'As soon as you eat from the tree, your eyes will be opened, and you shall become like gods, knowing good and evil.' But look! He has burnt your bodies with fire, and has made you taste the taste of fire, for the taste of the garden; and has made you see the burning of fire, and the evil of it, and the power it has over you.

7 Your eyes have seen the good he has taken from you, and in truth he has opened your eyes; and you have seen the garden in which you were with Me, and you have also seen the evil that has come over you from Satan. But as to the Godhead he cannot give it to you, neither fulfil his speech to you. No, he was bitter against you and your descendants, that will come after you."

8 And God withdrew His Word form them.

* At this time, the garments that the Lord had given them in Genesis 3:21 were burned off so that Adam and Eve were again naked. Reference chapter L whereby Adam and Eve seek garments with which to cover their nakedness..

Chapter XLVII - The Devil's own Scheming.

1 Then Adam and Eve came into the cave, yet trembling at the fire that had scorched their bodies. So Adam said to Eve:—

2 "Look, the fire has burnt our flesh in this world; but how will it be when we are dead, and Satan shall punish our souls? Is not our deliverance long and far off, unless God come, and in mercy to us fulfil His promise?"

3 Then Adam and Eve passed into the cave, blessing themselves for coming into it once more. For it was in their thoughts, that they never should enter it, when they saw the fire around it.

4 But as the sun was setting the fire was still burning and nearing Adam and Eve in the cave, so that they could not sleep in it. After the sun had set, they went out of it. This was the forty-seventh day after they came out of the garden.

5 Adam and Eve then came under the top of hill by the garden to sleep, as they were accustomed.

6 And they stood and prayed God to forgive them their sins, and then fell asleep under the summit of the mountain.

7 But Satan, the hater of all good, thought within himself: "Whereas God has promised salvation to Adam by covenant, and that He would deliver him out of all the hardships that have befallen him—but has not promised me by covenant, and will not deliver me out of my hardships; no, since He has promised him that He should make him and his descendants live in the kingdom in which I once was—I will kill Adam.

8 The earth shall be rid of him; and shall be left to me alone; so that when he is dead he may not have any descendants left to inherit the kingdom that shall remain my own realm; God will then be wanting me, and He will restore it to me and my hosts."

Chapter XLVIII - Fifth apparition of Satan to Adam and Eve.

1 After this Satan called to his hosts, all of which came to him, and said to him:—

2 "O, our lord, what will you do?"

3 He then said to them, "You know that this Adam, whom God created out of the dust, is the one who has taken our kingdom, come, let us gather together and kill him; or hurl a rock at him and at Eve, and crush them under it."

4 When Satan's hosts heard these words, they came to the part of the mountain where Adam and Eve were asleep.

5 Then Satan and his host took a huge rock, broad and even, and without blemish, thinking within himself, "If there should be a hole in the rock, when it fell on them, the hole in the rock might come over them, and so they would escape and not die."

6 He then said to his hosts, "Take up this stone, and throw it flat on them, so that it doesn't roll off them to somewhere else. And when you have hurled it, get away from there quickly."

7 And they did as he told them. But as the rock fell down from the mountain toward Adam and Eve, God commanded the rock to become a dome over them*, that did them no harm. And so it was by God's order.

8 But when the rock fell, the whole earth quaked with it**, and was shaken from the size of the rock.

9 And as it quaked and shook, Adam and Eve awoke from sleep, and found themselves under a dome of rock. But they didn't know what had happened; because when the fell asleep they were under the sky, and not under a dome; and when they saw it, they were afraid.

10 Then Adam said to Eve, "Wherefore has the mountain bent itself, and the earth quaked and shaken on our account? And why has this rock spread itself over us like a tent?

11 Does God intend to plague us and to shut us up in this prison? Or will He close the earth over us?

12 He is angry with us for our having come out of the cave, without His order; and for our having done so of our own accord, without consulting Him, when we left the cave and came to this place."

13 Then Eve said, "If, indeed, the earth quaked for our sake, and this rock forms a tent over us because of our transgression, then we will be sorry, O Adam, because our punishment will be long.

14 But get up and pray to God to let us know concerning this, and what this rock is that is spread over us like a tent."

15 Then Adam stood up and prayed before the Lord, to let him know what had brought about this difficult time. And Adam stood praying like that until the morning.

* The word "dome" is used here but the text does not specifically suggest that the covering was round—only that it covered them on all sides, however a dome is the most likely shape that would have be able to withstand the impact with the ground. From verse 9 that says "when they saw it" and verse 11 that says "shut us up in this prison", we can conclude that the dome had holes in its sides that were big enough to let in light and air but were too small to allow Adam and Eve to escape. Another conclusion would be that the holes were large but too high up for Adam and Eve to reach, however the former is more likely.

** In verse 7 of the next chapter (XLIX), God tells Adam and Eve that the ground was also lowered under them—"I commanded ... the rock under you to lower itself".

Chapter XLIX - The first prophecy of the Resurrection.

1 Then the Word of God came and said:—

2 "O Adam, who counselled you, when you came out of the cave, to come to this place?"

3 And Adam said to God, "O Lord, we came to this place because of the heat of the fire, that came over us inside the cave."

4 Then the Lord God said to Adam, "O Adam, you dread the heat of fire for one night, but how will it be when you live in hell?

5 Yet, O Adam, don't be afraid, and don't believe that I have placed this dome of rock over you to plague you with it.

6 It came from Satan, who had promised you the Godhead and majesty. It is he who threw down this rock to kill you under it, and Eve with you, and thus to prevent you from living on the earth.

7 But, in mercy for you, just as that rock was falling down on you, I commanded it to form an dome over you; and the rock under you to lower itself.

8 And this sign, O Adam, will happen to Me at My coming on earth: Satan will raise the people of the Jews to put Me to death; and they will lay Me in a rock, and seal a large stone over Me, and I shall remain within that rock three days and three nights.

9 But on the third day I shall rise again, and it shall be salvation to you, O Adam, and to your descendants, to believe in Me. But, O Adam, I will not bring you from under this rock until three days and three nights have passed."

10 And God withdrew His Word from Adam.

11 But Adam and Eve lived under the rock three days and three nights, as God had told them.

12 And God did so to them because they had left their cave and had come to this same place without God's order.

13 But, after three days and three nights, God created an opening in the dome of rock and allowed them to get out from under it. Their flesh was dried up, and their eyes and hearts were troubled from crying and sorrow.

Chapter L - Adam and Eve seek to cover their nakedness.

1 Then Adam and Eve went forth and came into the Cave of Treasures, and they stood praying in it the whole of that day, until the evening.

2 And this took place at the end of the fifty days after they had left the garden.

3 But Adam and Eve rose again and prayed to God in the cave the whole of that night, and begged for mercy from Him.

4 And when the day dawned, Adam said to Eve, "Come! Let us go and do some work for our bodies."

5 So they went out of the cave, and came to the northern border of the garden, and they looked for something to cover their bodies with*. But they found nothing, and knew not how to do the work. Yet their bodies were stained, and they were speechless from cold and heat.

6 Then Adam stood and asked God to show him something with which to cover their bodies.

7 Then came the Word of God and said to him, "O Adam, take Eve and come to the seashore where you fasted before. There you will find skins of sheep that were left after lions ate the carcasses. Take them and make garments for yourselves, and clothe yourselves with them.

* Chapter XLVI, verse 1, says "Satan blew into the fire ... so that their bodies were singed". At this time, the garments that the Lord had given them in Genesis 3:21 were burned off so that Adam and Eve were again naked.

Chapter LI - "What is his beauty that you should have followed him?"

1 When Adam heard these words from God, he took Eve and went from the northern end of the garden to the south of it, by the river of water where they once fasted.

2 But as they were going on their way, and before they got there, Satan, the wicked one, had heard the Word of God communing with Adam respecting his covering.

3 It grieved him, and he hastened to the place where the sheep-skins were, with the intention of taking them and throwing them into the sea, or of burning them with fire, so that Adam and Eve would not find them.

4 But as he was about to take them, the Word of God came from heaven, and bound him by the side of those skins until Adam and Eve came near him. But as they got closer to him they were afraid of him, and of his hideous look.

5 Then came the Word of God to Adam and Eve, and said to them, "This is he who was hidden in the serpent, and who deceived you, and stripped you of the garment of light and glory in which you were.

6 This is he who promised you majesty and divinity. Where, then, is the beauty that was on him? Where is his divinity? Where is his light? Where is the glory that rested on him?

7 Now his figure is hideous; he is become abominable among angels; and he has come to be called Satan.

8 O Adam, he wished to take from you this earthly garment of sheep-skins, and to destroy it, and not let you be covered with it.

9 What, then, is his beauty that you should have followed him? And what have you gained by obeying him? See his evil works and then look at Me; at Me, your Creator, and at the good deeds I do you.

10 See, I bound him until you came and saw him and beheld his weakness, that no power is left with him."

11 And God released him from his bonds.

Chapter LII - Adam and Eve sew the first shirt.

1 After this Adam and Eve said no more, but cried before God on account of their creation, and of their bodies that required an earthly covering.

2 Then Adam said to Eve, "O Eve, this is the skin of beasts with which we shall be covered, but when we put it on, behold, we shall be wearing a token of death on our bodies. Just as the owners of these skins have died and have wasted away, so also shall we die and pass away."

3 Then Adam and Eve took the skins, and went back to the Cave of Treasures; and when in it, they stood and prayed as they were accustomed.

4 And they thought how they could make garments of those skins; for they had no skill for it.

5 Then God sent to them His angel to show them how to work it out. And the angel said to Adam, "Go forth, and bring some palm-thorns." Then Adam went out, and brought some, as the angel had commanded him.

6 Then the angel began before them to work out the skins, after the manner of one who prepares a shirt. And he took the thorns and stuck them into the skins, before their eyes.

7 Then the angel again stood up and prayed God that the thorns in those skins should be hidden, so as to be, as it were, sewn with one thread.

8 And so it was, by God's order; they became garments for Adam and Eve, and He clothed them therewith.

9 From that time the nakedness of their bodies was covered from the sight of each other's eyes.

10 And this happened at the end of the fifty-first day.

11 Then when Adam's and Eve's bodies were covered, they stood and prayed, and sought mercy of the Lord, and forgiveness, and gave Him thanks for that He had had mercy on

them, and had covered their nakedness. And they ceased not from prayer the whole of that night.

12 Then when the morning dawned at the rising of the sun, they said their prayers after their custom; and then went out of the cave.

13 And Adam said to Eve, "Since we don't know what there is to the west of this cave, let us go out and see it today." Then they came forth and went toward the western border.

Chapter LIII - The prophecy of the Western Lands and of the great flood.

1 They were not very far from the cave, when Satan came towards them, and hid himself between them and the cave, under the form of two ravenous lions three days without food, that came towards Adam and Eve, as if to break them in pieces and devour them.

2 Then Adam and Eve cried, and prayed God to deliver them from their paws.

3 Then the Word of God came to them, and drove away the lions from them.

4 And God said to Adam, "O Adam, what do you seek on the western border? And why have you left of thine own accord the eastern border, in which was your living place?

5 Now then, turn back to your cave, and remain in it, so that Satan won't deceive you or work his purpose over you.

6 For in this western border, O Adam, there will go from you a descendant, that shall replenish it; and that will defile themselves with their sins, and with their yielding to the commands of Satan, and by following his works.

7 Therefore will I bring over them the waters of a flood, and overwhelm them all. But I will deliver what is left of the righteous among them; and I will bring them to a distant land, and the land in which you live now shall remain desolate and without one inhabitant in it.

8 After God had thus spoken to them, they went back to the Cave of Treasures. But their flesh was dried up, and they were weak from fasting and praying, and from the sorrow they felt at having trespassed against God.

Chapter LIV - Adam and Eve go exploring.

1 Then Adam and Eve stood up in the cave and prayed the whole of that night until the morning dawned. And when the sun was risen they both went out of the cave; their heads were wandering from heaviness of sorrow and they didn't know where they were going.

2 And they walked in that condition to the southern border of the garden. And they began to go up that border until they came to the eastern border beyond which there was no more land.

3 And the cherub who guarded the garden was standing at the western gate, and guarding it against Adam and Eve, lest they should suddenly come into the garden. And the cherub turned around, as if to put them to death; according to the commandment God had given him.

4 When Adam and Eve came to the eastern border of the garden—thinking in their hearts that the cherub was not watching—as they were standing by the gate as if wishing to go in, suddenly came the cherub with a flashing sword of fire in his hand; and when he saw them, he went forth to kill them. For he was afraid that God would destroy him if they went into the garden without His order.

5 And the sword of the cherub seemed to shoot flames a distance away from it. But when he raised it over Adam and Eve, the flame of the sword did not flash forth.

6 Therefore the cherub thought that God was favorable to them, and was bringing them back into the garden. And the cherub stood wondering.

7 He could not go up to Heaven to determine God's order regarding their getting into the garden; he therefore continued to stand by them, unable as he was to part from them; for he was afraid that if they should enter the garden without permission, God would destroy him.

8 When Adam and Eve saw the cherub coming towards them with a flaming sword of fire in his hand, they fell on their faces from fear, and were as dead.

9 At that time the heavens and the earth shook; and another cherubim came down from heaven to the cherub who guarded the garden, and saw him amazed and silent.

10 Then, again, other angels came down close to the place where Adam and Eve were. They were divided between joy and sorrow.

11 They were glad, because they thought that God was favorable to Adam, and wished him to return to the garden; and wished to restore him to the gladness he once enjoyed.

12 But they sorrowed over Adam, because he was fallen like a dead man, he and Eve; and they said in their thoughts, "Adam has not died in this place; but God has put him to death, for his having come to this place, and wishing to get into the garden without His permission."

Chapter LV - The Conflict between God and Satan.

1 Then came the Word of God to Adam and Eve, and raised them from their dead state, saying to them, "Why did you come up here? Do you intend to go into the garden, from

which I brought you out? It cannot be today; but only when the covenant I have made with you is fulfilled."

2 Then Adam, when he heard the Word of God, and the fluttering of the angels whom he did not see, but only heard the sound of them with his ears, he and Eve cried, and said to the angels:—

3 "O Spirits, who wait on God, look at me, and at my being unable to see you! For when I was in my former bright nature, then I could see you. I sang praises as you do; and my heart was far above you.

4 But now, that I have transgressed, that bright nature is gone from me, and I am come to this miserable state. And now I have come to this, that I cannot see you, and you do not serve me like you used to do. For I have become animal flesh.

5 Yet now, O angels of God, ask God with me, to restore me to that wherein I was formerly; to rescue me from this misery, and to remove from me the sentence of death He passed on me, for having trespassed against Him."

6 Then, when the angels heard these words, they all grieved over him; and cursed Satan who had misled Adam, until he came from the garden to misery; from life to death; from peace to trouble; and from gladness to a strange land.

7 Then the angels said to Adam, "You obeyed Satan, and ignored the Word of God who created you; and you believed that Satan would fulfil all he had promised you.

8 But now, O Adam, we will make known to you, what came over us though him, before his fall from heaven.

9 He gathered together his hosts, and deceived them, promising to give them a great kingdom, a divine nature; and other promises he made them.

10 His hosts believed that his word was true, so they yielded to him, and renounced the glory of God.

11 He then sent for us—according to the orders in which we were—to come under his command, and to accept his vein promise. But we would not, and we did not take his advice.

12 Then after he had fought with God, and had dealt forwardly with Him, he gathered together his hosts, and made war with us. And if it had not been for God's strength that was with us, we could not have prevailed against him to hurl him from heaven.

13 But when he fell from among us, there was great joy in heaven, because of his going down from us. For if he had remained in heaven, nothing, not even one angel would have remained in it.

14 But God in His mercy, drove him from among us to this dark earth; for he had become darkness itself and a worker of unrighteousness.

15 And he has continued, O Adam, to make war against you, until he tricked you and made you come out of the garden, to this strange land, where all these trials have come to you.

And death, which God brought to him, he has also brought to you, O Adam, because you obeyed him, and trespassed against God."

16 Then all the angels rejoiced and praised God, and asked Him not to destroy Adam this time, for his having sought to enter the garden; but to bear with him until the fulfillment of the promise; and to help him in this world until he was free from Satan's hand.

Chapter LVI - A chapter of divine comfort.

1 Then came the Word of God to Adam, and said to him:—

2 "O Adam, look at that garden of joy and at this earth of toil, and behold the garden is full of angels, but look at yourself alone on this earth with Satan whom you obeyed.

3 Yet, if you had submitted, and been obedient to Me, and had kept My Word, you would be with My angels in My garden.

4 But when you transgressed and obeyed Satan, you became his guests among his angels, that are full of wickedness; and you came to this earth, that brings forth to you thorns and thistles.

5 O Adam, ask him who deceived you, to give you the divine nature he promised you, or to make you a garden as I had made for you; or to fill you with that same bright nature with which I had filled you.

6 Ask him to make you a body like the one I made you, or to give you a day of rest as I gave you; or to create within you a reasonable soul, as I created for you; or to take you from here to some other earth than this one which I gave you. But, O Adam, he will not fulfil even one of the things he told you.

7 Acknowledge, then, My favor towards you, and My mercy on you, My creature; that I have not avenged you for your transgression against Me, but in My pity for you I have promised you that at the end of the great five and a half days I will come and save you."

8 Then God said again to Adam and Eve, "Get up, go down from here, before the cherub with a sword of fire in his hand destroys you."

9 But Adam's heart was comforted by God's words to him, and he worshipped before Him.

10 And God commanded His angels to escort Adam and Eve to the cave with joy, instead of the fear that had come over them.

11 Then the angels took up Adam and Eve, and brought them down from the mountain by the garden, with songs and psalms, until they arrived at the cave. There the angels began to comfort and to strengthen them, and then departed from them towards heaven, to their Creator, who had sent them.

12 But after the angels had departed from Adam and Eve, Satan came with shamefacedness, and stood at the entrance of the cave in which were Adam and Eve. He then called to Adam, and said, "O Adam, come, let me speak to you."

13 Then Adam came out of the cave, thinking he was one of God's angels that was come to give him some good counsel.

Chapter LVII - "Therefore I fell.... "

1 But when Adam came out and saw his hideous figure, he was afraid of him, and said to him, "Who are you?"

2 Then Satan answered and said to him, "It is I, who hid myself within the serpent, and who spoke to Eve, and who enticed her until she obeyed my command. I am he who sent her, using my deceitful speech, to deceive you, until you both ate of the fruit of the tree and abandoned the command of God."

3 But when Adam heard these words from him, he said to him, "Can you make me a garden as God made for me? Or can you clothe me in the same bright nature in which God had clothed me?

4 Where is the divine nature you promised to give me? Where is that slick speech of yours that you had with us at first, when we were in the garden?"

5 Then Satan said to Adam, "Do you think that when I have promised one something that I would actually deliver it to him or fulfil my word? Of course not. For I myself have never even thought of obtaining what I promised.

6 Therefore I fell, and I made you fall by that for which I myself fell; and with you also, whosoever accepts my counsel, falls thereby.

7 But now, O Adam, because you fell you are under my rule, and I am king over you; because you have obeyed me and have transgressed against your God. Neither will there be any deliverance from my hands until the day promised you by your God."

8 Again he said, "Because we do not know the day agreed on with you by your God, nor the hour in which you shall be delivered, for that reason we will multiply war and murder on you and your descendants after you.

9 This is our will and our good pleasure, that we may not leave one of the sons of men to inherit our orders in heaven.

10 For as to our home, O Adam, it is in burning fire; and we will not stop our evil doing, no, not one day nor one hour. And I, O Adam, shall set you on fire when you come into the cave to live there."

11 When Adam heard these words he cried and mourned, and said to Eve, "Hear what he said; that he won't fulfil any of what he told you in the garden. Did he really then become king over us?

12 But we will ask God, who created us, to deliver us out of his hands."

Chapter LVIII - "About sunset on the 53rd day..."

1 Then Adam and Eve spread their hands before God, praying and begging Him to drive Satan away from them so that he can't harm them or force them to deny God.

2 Then God sent to them at once, His angel, who drove away Satan from them. This happened about sunset, on the fifty-third day after they had come out of the garden.

3 Then Adam and Eve went into the cave, and stood up and turned their faces to the ground, to pray to God.

4 But before they prayed Adam said to Eve, "Look, you have seen what temptations have befallen us in this land. Come, let us get up, and ask God to forgive us the sins we have committed; and we will not come out until the end of the day next to the fortieth. And if we die in here, He will save us."

5 Then Adam and Eve got up, and joined together in entreating God.

6 They continued praying like this in the cave; neither did they come out of it, by night or by day, until their prayers went up out of their mouths, like a flame of fire.

Chapter LIX - Eighth apparition of Satan of Satan to Adam and Eve.

1 But Satan, the hater of all good, did not allow them to finish their prayers. For he called to his hosts, and they came, all of them. Then he said to them, "Since Adam and Eve, whom we deceived, have agreed together to pray to God night and day, and to beg Him to deliver them, and since they will not come out of the cave until the end of the fortieth day.

2 And since they will continue their prayers as they have both agreed to do, that He will deliver them out of our hands, and restore them to their former state, see what we shall do to them." And his hosts said to him, "Power is thine, O our lord, to do what you list."

3 Then Satan, great in wickedness, took his hosts and came into the cave, in the thirtieth night of the forty days and one; and he beat Adam and Eve, until he left them dead.

4 Then came the Word of God to Adam and Eve, who raised them from their suffering, and God said to Adam, "Be strong, and be not afraid of him who has just come to you."

5 But Adam cried and said, "Where were you, O my God, that they should punish me with such blows, and that this suffering should come over us; over me and over Eve, Your handmaiden?"

6 Then God said to him, "O Adam, see, he is lord and master of all you have, he who said, he would give you divinity. Where is this love for you? And where is the gift he promised?

7 Did it please him just once, O Adam, to come to you, comfort you, strengthen you, rejoice with you, or send his hosts to protect you; because you have obeyed him, and have yielded to his counsel; and have followed his commandment and transgressed Mine?"

8 Then Adam cried before the Lord, and said, "O Lord because I transgressed a little, You have severely punished me in return for it, I ask You to deliver me out of his hands; or else have pity on me, and take my soul out of my body now in this strange land."

9 Then God said to Adam, "If only there had been this sighing and praying before, before you transgressed! Then would you have rest from the trouble in which you are now."

10 But God had patience with Adam, and let him and Eve remain in the cave until they had fulfilled the forty days.

11 But as to Adam and Eve, their strength and flesh withered from fasting and praying, from hunger and thirst; for they had not tasted either food or drink since they left the garden; nor were the functions of their bodies yet settled; and they had no strength left to continue in prayer from hunger, until the end of the next day to the fortieth. They were fallen down in the cave; yet what speech escaped from their mouths, was only in praises.

Chapter LX - The Devil appears like an old man. He offers "a place of rest."

1 Then on the eighty-ninth day, Satan came to the cave, clad in a garment of light, and girt about with a bright girdle.

2 In his hands was a staff of light, and he looked most awful; but his face was pleasant and his speech was sweet.

3 He thus transformed himself in order to deceive Adam and Eve, and to make them come out of the cave, before they had fulfilled the forty days.

4 For he said within himself, "Now that when they had fulfilled the forty days' fasting and praying, God would restore them to their former state; but if He did not do so, He would still be favorable to them; and even if He had not mercy on them, would He yet give them something from the garden to comfort them; as already twice before."

5 Then Satan drew near the cave in this fair appearance, and said:—

6 "O Adam, get up, stand up, you and Eve, and come along with me, to a good land; and don't be afraid. I am flesh and bones like you; and at first I was a creature that God created.

7 And it was so, that when He had created me, He placed me in a garden in the north, on the border of the world.

8 And He said to me, 'Stay here!' And I remained there according to His Word, neither did I transgress His commandment.

9 Then He made a slumber to come over me, and He brought you, O Adam, out of my side, but did not make you stay with me.

10 But God took you in His divine hand, and placed you in a garden to the eastward.

11 Then I worried about you, for that while God had taken you out of my side, He had not let you stay with me.

12 But God said to me: 'Do not worry about Adam, whom I brought out of your side; no harm will come to him.

13 For now I have brought out of his side a help-meet* for him; and I have given him joy by so doing.'"

14 Then Satan said again, "I did not know how it is you are in this cave, nor anything about this trial that has come over you—until God said to me, 'Behold, Adam has transgressed, he whom I had taken out of your side, and Eve also, whom I took out of his side; and I have driven them out of the garden; I have made them live in a land of sorrow and misery, because they transgressed against Me, and have obeyed Satan. And look, they are in suffering until this day, the eightieth.'

15 Then God said to me, 'Get up, go to them, and make them come to your place, and suffer not that Satan come near them, and afflict them. For they are now in great misery; and lie helpless from hunger.'

16 He further said to me, 'When you have taken them to yourself, give them to eat of the fruit of the Tree of Life, and give them to drink of the water of peace; and clothe them in a garment of light, and restore them to their former state of grace, and leave them not in misery, for they came from you. But grieve not over them, nor repent of that which has come over them.

17 But when I heard this, I was sorry; and my heart could not patiently bear it for your sake, O my child.

18 But, O Adam, when I heard the name of Satan, I was afraid, and I said within myself, I will not come out because he might trap me as he did my children, Adam and Eve.

19 And I said, 'O God, when I go to my children, Satan will meet me in the way, and war against me, as he did against them.'

20 Then God said to me, 'Fear not; when you find him, hit him with the staff that is in thine hand, and don't be afraid of him, for you are of old standing, and he shall not prevail against you.'

21 Then I said, 'O my Lord, I am old, and cannot go. Send Your angels to bring them.'

22 But God said to me, 'Angels, verily, are not like them; and they will not consent to come with them. But I have chosen you, because they are your offspring and are like you, and they will listen to what you say.'

23 God said further to me, 'If you don't have enough strength to walk, I will send a cloud to carry you and set you down at the entrance of their cave; then the cloud will return and leave you there.

24 And if they will come with you, I will send a cloud to carry you and them.'

25 Then He commanded a cloud, and it bear me up and brought me to you; and then went back.

26 And now, O my children, Adam and Eve, look at my old gray hair and at my feeble state, and at my coming from that distant place. Come, come with me, to a place of rest."

27 Then he began to cry and to sob before Adam and Eve, and his tears poured on the ground like water.

28 And when Adam and Eve raised their eyes and saw his beard, and heard his sweet talk, their hearts softened towards him; they obeyed him, for they believed he was true.

29 And it seemed to them that they were really his offspring, when they saw that his face was like their own; and they trusted him.

* The existence of the two words helpmeet and helpmate, meaning exactly the same thing, is a comedy of errors. God's promise to Adam, as rendered in the King James version of the Bible, was to give him an help meet for him (that is, a helper fit for him). In the 17th century the two words help and meet in this passage were mistaken for one word, applying to Eve, and thus helpmeet came to mean a wife. Then in the 18th century, in a misguided attempt to make sense of the word, the spelling helpmate was introduced. Both errors are now beyond recall, and both spellings are acceptable.

Chapter LXI - They begin to follow Satan.

1 Then he took Adam and Eve by the hand, and began to bring them out of the cave.

2 But when they had come a little ways out of it, God knew that Satan had overcome them, and had brought them out before the forty days were ended, to take them to some distant place, and to destroy them.

3 Then the Word of the Lord God again came and cursed Satan, and drove him away from them.

4 And God began to speak to Adam and Eve, saying to them, "What made you come out of the cave, to this place?"

5 Then Adam said to God, "Did you create a man before us? For when we were in the cave there suddenly came to us a friendly old man who said to us, 'I am a messenger from God to you, to bring you back to some place of rest.'

6 And we believed, O God, that he was a messenger from you; and we came out with him; and knew not where we should go with him."

7 Then God said to Adam, "See, that is the father of evil arts, who brought you and Eve out of the Garden of Delights. And now, indeed, when he saw that you and Eve both joined together in fasting and praying, and that you came not out of the cave before the end of the forty days, he wished to make your purpose vein, to break your mutual bond; to cut off all hope from you, and to drive you to some place where he might destroy you.

8 Because he couldn't do anything to you unless he showed himself in the likeness of you.

9 Therefore he came to you with a face like your own, and began to give you tokens as if they were all true.

10 But because I am merciful and am favorable to you, I did not allow him to destroy you; instead I drove him away from you.

11 Now, therefore, O Adam, take Eve, and return to your cave, and remain in it until the morning after the fortieth day. And when you come out, go towards the eastern gate of the garden."

12 Then Adam and Eve worshipped God, and praised and blessed Him for the deliverance that had come to them from Him. And they returned towards the cave. This happened in the evening of the thirty-ninth day.

13 Then Adam and Eve stood up and with a fiery passion, prayed to God, to give them strength; for they had become weak because of hunger and thirst and prayer. But they watched the whole of that night praying, until morning.

14 Then Adam said to Eve, "Get up, let us go towards the eastern gate of the garden as God told us."

15 And they said their prayers as they were accustomed to do every day; and they left the cave to go near to the eastern gate of the garden.

16 Then Adam and Eve stood up and prayed, and appealed to God to strengthen them, and to send them something to satisfy their hunger.

17 But after they finished their prayers, they were too weak to move.

18 Then came the Word of God again, and said to them, "O Adam, get up, go and bring the two figs here."

19 Then Adam and Eve got up, and went until they came near to the cave.

Chapter LXII - Two fruit trees.

1 But Satan the wicked was envious, because of the consolation God had given them.

2 So he prevented them, and went into the cave and took the two figs, and buried them outside the cave, so that Adam and Eve should not find them. He also had in his thoughts to destroy them.

3 But by God's mercy, as soon as those two figs were in the ground, God defeated Satan's counsel regarding them; and made them into two fruit trees, that overshadowed the cave. For Satan had buried them on the eastern side of it.

4 Then when the two trees were grown, and were covered with fruit, Satan grieved and mourned, and said, "It would have been better to have left those figs where they were; for now, behold, they have become two fruit trees, whereof Adam will eat all the days of his life. Whereas I had in mind, when I buried them, to destroy them entirely, and to hide them forever.

5 But God has overturned my counsel; and would not that this sacred fruit should perish; and He has made plain my intention, and has defeated the counsel I had formed against His servants."

6 Then Satan went away ashamed because he hadn't thought his plans all the way through.

Chapter LXIII - The first joy of trees.

1 But Adam and Eve, as they got closer to the cave, saw two fig trees, covered with fruit, and overshadowing the cave.

2 Then Adam said to Eve, "It seems to me that we have gone the wrong way. When did these two trees grow here? It seems to me that the enemy wishes to lead us the wrong way. Do you suppose that there is another cave besides this one in the earth?

3 Yet, O Eve, let us go into the cave, and find in it the two figs; for this is our cave, in which we were. But if we should not find the two figs in it, then it cannot be our cave."

4 They went then into the cave, and looked into the four corners of it, but found not the two figs.

5 And Adam cried and said to Eve, "Did we go to the wrong cave, then, O Eve? It seems to me these two fig trees are the two figs that were in the cave." And Eve said, "I, for my part, do not know."

6 Then Adam stood up and prayed and said, "O God, You commanded us to come back to the cave, to take the two figs, and then to return to you.

7 But now, we have not found them. O God, have you taken them, and sown these two trees, or have we gone astray in the earth; or has the enemy deceived us? If it be real, then, O God, reveal to us the secret of these two trees and of the two figs."

8 Then came the Word of God to Adam, and said to him, "O Adam, when I sent you to fetch the figs, Satan went before you to the cave, took the figs, and buried them outside, eastward of the cave, thinking to destroy them; and not sowing them with good intent.

9 Not for his mere sake, then, have these trees grown up at once; but I had mercy on you and I commanded them to grow. And they grew to be two large trees, that you be overshadowed by their branches, and find rest; and that I made you see My power and My marvelous works.

10 And, also, to show you Satan's meanness, and his evil works, for ever since you came out of the garden, he has not ceased, no, not one day, from doing you some harm. But I have not given him power over you."

11 And God said, "From now on, O Adam, rejoice on account of the trees, you and Eve; and rest under them when you feel weary. But do not eat any of their fruit or come near them."

12 Then Adam cried, and said, "O God, will You again kill us, or will You drive us away from before Your face, and cut our life from off the face of the earth?

13 O God, I beg you, if You know that there be in these trees either death or some other evil, as at the first time, root them up from near our cave, and with them; and leave us to die of the heat, of hunger and of thirst.

14 For we know Your marvelous works, O God, that they are great, and that by Your power You can bring one thing out of another, without one's wish. For Your power can make rocks to become trees, and trees to become rocks."

Chapter LXIV - Adam and Eve partake of the first earthly food.

1 Then God looked at Adam and at his strength of mind, at his endurance of hunger and thirst, and of the heat. And He changed the two fig trees into two figs, as they were at first, and then said to Adam and to Eve, "Each of you may take one fig." And they took them, as the Lord commanded them.

2 And He said to them, "You must now go into the cave and eat the figs, and satisfy your hunger, or else you will die."

3 So, as God commanded them, they went into the cave about sunset. And Adam and Eve stood up and prayed during the setting sun.

4 Then they sat down to eat the figs; but they knew not how to eat them; for they were not accustomed to eat earthly food. They were afraid that if they ate, their stomach would be burdened and their flesh thickened, and their hearts would take to liking earthly food.

5 But while they were thus seated, God, out of pity for them, sent them His angel, so they wouldn't perish of hunger and thirst.

6 And the angel said to Adam and Eve, "God says to you that you do not have the strength that would be required to fast until death; eat, therefore, and strengthen your bodies; for you are now animal flesh and cannot subsist without food and drink."

7 Then Adam and Eve took the figs and began to eat of them. But God had put into them a mixture as of savory bread and blood.

8 Then the angel went from Adam and Eve, who ate of the figs until they had satisfied their hunger. Then they put aside what was left; but by the power of God, the figs became whole again, because God blessed them.

9 After this Adam and Eve got up, and prayed with a joyful heart and renewed strength, and praised and rejoiced abundantly the whole of that night. And this was the end of the eighty-third day.

Chapter LXV - Adam and Eve acquire digestive organs. Final hope of returning to the Garden is lost.

1 And when it was day, they got up and prayed, after their custom, and then went out of the cave.

2 But they became sick from the food they had eaten because they were not used to it, so they went about in the cave saying to each other:—

3 "What has our eating caused to happen to us, that we should be in such pain? We are in misery, we shall die! It would have been better for us to have died keeping our bodies pure than to have eaten and defiled them with food."

4 Then Adam said to Eve, "This pain did not come to us in the garden, neither did we eat such bad food there. Do you think, O Eve, that God will plague us through the food that is in us, or that our innards will come out; or that God means to kill us with this pain before He has fulfilled His promise to us?"

5 Then Adam besought the Lord and said, "O Lord, let us not perish through the food we have eaten. O Lord, don't punish us; but deal with us according to Your great mercy, and forsake us not until the day of the promise You have made us."

6 Then God looked at them, and then fitted them for eating food at once; as to this day; so that they should not perish.

7 Then Adam and Eve came back into the cave sorrowful and crying because of the alteration of their bodies. And they both knew from that hour that they were altered beings, that all hope of returning to the garden was now lost; and that they could not enter it.

8 For that now their bodies had strange functions; and all flesh that requires food and drink for its existence, cannot be in the garden.

9 Then Adam said to Eve, "Behold, our hope is now lost; and so is our trust to enter the garden. We no longer belong to the inhabitants of the garden; but from now on we are earthy and of the dust, and of the inhabitants of the earth. We shall not return to the garden, until the day in which God has promised to save us, and to bring us again into the garden, as He promised us."

10 Then they prayed to God that He would have mercy on them; after which, their mind was quieted, their hearts were broken, and their longing was cooled down; and they were like strangers on earth. That night Adam and Eve spent in the cave, where they slept heavily by reason of the food they had eaten.

Chapter LXVI - Adam does his first day's work.

1 When it was morning, the day after they had eaten food, Adam and Eve prayed in the cave, and Adam said to Eve, "Look, we asked for food of God, and He gave it. But now let us also ask Him to give us a drink of water."

2 Then they got up, and went to the bank of the stream of water, that was on the south border of the garden, in which they had before thrown themselves. And they stood on the bank, and prayed to God that He would command them to drink of the water.

3 Then the Word of God came to Adam, and said to him, "O Adam, your body has become brutish, and requires water to drink. Take some and drink it, you and Eve, then give thanks and praise."

4 Adam and Eve then went down to the stream and drank from it, until their bodies felt refreshed. After having drunk, they praised God, and then returned to their cave, after their former custom. This happened at the end of eighty-three days.

5 Then on the eighty-fourth day, they took the two figs and hung them in the cave, together with the leaves thereof, to be to them a sign and a blessing from God. And they placed them there so that if their descendants came there, they would see the wonderful things God had done for them.

6 Then Adam and Eve again stood outside the cave, and asked God to show them some food with which they could nourish their bodies.

7 Then the Word of God came and said to him, "O Adam, go down to the westward of the cave until you come to a land of dark soil, and there you shall find food."

8 And Adam obeyed the Word of God, took Eve, and went down to a land of dark soil, and found there wheat* growing in the ear and ripe, and figs to eat; and Adam rejoiced over it.

9 Then the Word of God came again to Adam, and said to him, "Take some of this wheat and make yourselves some bread with it, to nourish your body therewith." And God gave Adam's heart wisdom, to work out the corn until it became bread.

10 Adam accomplished all that, until he grew very faint and weary. He then returned to the cave; rejoicing at what he had learned of what is done with wheat, until it is made into bread for one's use.

* In this book, the terms 'corn' and 'wheat' are used interchangeably. The reference is possibly used to indicate a type of ancient grain resembling Egyptian Corn also known as Durra. Durra is a wheat-like cereal grain frequently cultivated in dry regions such as Egypt.

Chapter LXVII - "Then Satan began to lead astray Adam and Eve...."

1 When Adam and Eve went down to the land of black mud and came near to the wheat God had showed them and saw that it was ripe and ready for reaping, they did not have a sickle to reap it with. So they readied themselves, and began to pull up the wheat by hand, until it was all done.

2 Then they heaped it into a pile; and, faint from heat and from thirst, they went under a shady tree, where the breeze fanned them to sleep.

3 But Satan saw what Adam and Eve had done. And he called his hosts, and said to them, "Since God has shown to Adam and Eve all about this wheat, wherewith to strengthen their bodies—and, look, they have come and made a big pile of it, and faint from the toil are now asleep—come, let us set fire to this heap of corn, and burn it, and let us take that bottle of water that is by them, and empty it out, so that they may find nothing to drink, and we kill them with hunger and thirst.

4 Then, when they wake up from their sleep, and seek to return to the cave, we will come to them in the way, and will lead them astray; so that they die of hunger and thirst; when they may, perhaps, deny God, and He destroy them. So shall we be rid of them."

5 Then Satan and his hosts set the wheat on fire and burned it up.

6 But from the heat of the flame Adam and Eve awoke from their sleep, and saw the wheat burning, and the bucket of water by them, poured out.

7 Then they cried and went back to the cave.

8 But as they were going up from below the mountain where they were, Satan and his hosts met them in the form of angels, praising God.

9 Then Satan said to Adam, "O Adam, why are you so pained with hunger and thirst? It seems to me that Satan has burnt up the wheat." And Adam said to him, "Yes."

10 Again Satan said to Adam, "Come back with us; we are angels of God. God sent us to you, to show you another field of corn, better than that; and beyond it is a fountain of good water, and many trees, where you shall live near it, and work the corn field to better purpose than that which Satan has consumed."

11 Adam thought that he was true, and that they were angels who talked with him; and he went back with them.

12 Then Satan began to lead astray Adam and Eve eight days, until they both fell down as if dead, from hunger, thirst, and faintness. Then he fled with his hosts, and left them.

Chapter LXVIII - How destruction and trouble is of Satan when he is the master. Adam and Eve establish the custom of worship.

1 Then God looked at Adam and Eve, and at what had come over them from Satan, and how he had made them perish.

2 God, therefore, sent His Word, and raised up Adam and Eve from their state of death.

3 Then, Adam, when he was raised, said, "O God, You have burnt and taken from us the corn You have given us, and You have emptied out the bucket of water. And You have sent Your angels, who have caused us to lose our way from the corn field. Will You make us perish? If this be from you, O God, then take away our souls; but punish us not."

4 Then God said to Adam, "I did not burn down the wheat, and I did not pour the water out of the bucket, and I did not send My angels to lead you astray.

5 But it is Satan, your master who did it; he to whom you have subjected yourself; my commandment being meanwhile set aside. He it is, who burnt down the corn, and poured out the water, and who has led you astray; and all the promises he has made you were just a trick, a deception, and a lie.

6 But now, O Adam, you shall acknowledge My good deeds done to you."

7 And God told His angels to take Adam and Eve, and to bear them up to the field of wheat, which they found as before, with the bucket full of water.

8 There they saw a tree, and found on it solid manna; and wondered at God's power. And the angels commanded them to eat of the manna when they were hungry.

9 And God admonished Satan with a curse, not to come again, and destroy the field of corn.

10 Then Adam and Eve took of the corn, and made of it an offering, and took it and offered it up on the mountain, the place where they had offered up their first offering of blood.

11 And they offered this offering again on the altar they had built at first. And they stood up and prayed, and besought the Lord saying, "Thus, O God, when we were in the garden, our praises went up to you, like this offering; and our innocence went up to you like incense. But now, O God, accept this offering from us, and don't turn us away, deprived of Your mercy."

12 Then God said to Adam and Eve, "Since you have made this offering and have offered it to Me, I shall make it My flesh, when I come down on earth to save you; and I shall cause it to be offered continually on an altar, for forgiveness and for mercy, for those who partake of it duly."

13 And God sent a bright fire over the offering of Adam and Eve, and filled it with brightness, grace, and light; and the Holy Ghost came down on that offering.

14 Then God commanded an angel to take fire tongs, like a spoon, and with it to take an offering and bring it to Adam and Eve. And the angel did so, as God had commanded him, and offered it to them.

15 And the souls of Adam and Eve were brightened, and their hearts were filled with joy and gladness and with the praises of God.

16 And God said to Adam, "This shall be to you a custom, to do so, when affliction and sorrow come over you. But your deliverance and your entrance in to the garden, shall not be until the days are fulfilled as agreed between you and Me; were it not so, I would, of My mercy and pity for you, bring you back to My garden and to My favor for the sake of the offering you have just made to My name."

17 Adam rejoiced at these words which he heard from God; and he and Eve worshipped before the altar, to which they bowed, and then went back to the Cave of Treasures.

18 And this took place at the end of the twelfth day after the eightieth day, from the time Adam and Eve came out of the garden.

19 And they stood up the whole night praying until morning; and then went out of the cave.

20 Then Adam said to Eve, with joy of heart, because of the offering they had made to God, and that had been accepted of Him, "Let us do this three times every week, on the fourth day Wednesday, on the preparation day Friday, and on the Sabbath Sunday, all the days of our life."

21 And as they agreed to these words between themselves, God was pleased with their thoughts, and with the resolution they had each taken with the other.

22 After this, came the Word of God to Adam, and said, "O Adam, you have determined beforehand the days in which sufferings shall come over Me, when I am made flesh; for they are the fourth Wednesday, and the preparation day Friday.

23 But as to the first day, I created in it all things, and I raised the heavens. And, again, through My rising again on this day, will I create joy, and raise them on high, who believe in Me; O Adam, offer this offering, all the days of your life."

24 Then God withdrew His Word from Adam.

25 But Adam continued to offer this offering thus, every week three times, until the end of seven weeks. And on the first day, which is the fiftieth, Adam made an offering as he was accustomed, and he and Eve took it and came to the altar before God, as He had taught them.

Chapter LXIX - Twelfth apparition of Satan to Adam and Eve, while Adam was praying over the offering on the altar; when Satan beat him.

1 Then Satan, the hater of all good, envious of Adam and of his offering through which he found favor with God, hastened and took a sharp stone from among the sharp iron stones; appeared in the form of a man, and went and stood by Adam and Eve.

2 Adam was then offering on the altar, and had begun to pray, with his hands spread before God.

3 Then Satan hastened with the sharp iron stone he had with him, and with it pierced Adam on the right side, from which flowed blood and water, then Adam fell on the altar like a corpse. And Satan fled.

4 Then Eve came, and took Adam and placed him below the altar. And there she stayed, crying over him; while a stream of blood flowed from Adam's side over his offering.

5 But God looked at the death of Adam. He then sent His Word, and raised him up and said to him, "Fulfil your offering, for indeed, Adam, it is worth much, and there is no shortcoming in it."

6 God said further to Adam, "Thus will it also happen to Me, on the earth, when I shall be pierced and blood and water shall flow from My side and run over My body, which is the true offering; and which shall be offered on the altar as a perfect offering."

7 Then God commanded Adam to finish his offering, and when he had ended it he worshipped before God, and praised Him for the signs He had showed him.

8 And God healed Adam in one day, which is the end of the seven weeks; and that is the fiftieth day.

9 Then Adam and Eve returned from the mountain, and went into the Cave of Treasures, as they were used to do. This completed for Adam and Eve, one hundred and forty days since their coming out of the garden.

10 Then they both stood up that night and prayed to God. And when it was morning, they went out, and went down westward of the cave, to the place where their corn was, and there rested under the shadow of a tree, as they were accustomed.

11 But when there a multitude of beasts came all around them. It was Satan's doing, in his wickedness; in order to wage war against Adam through marriage.

Chapter LXX - Thirteenth apparition of Satan, to trick Adam into marrying Eve.

1 After this Satan, the hater of all good, took the form of an angel, and with him two others, so that they looked like the three angels who had brought to Adam gold, incense, and myrrh.

2 They passed before Adam and Eve while they were under the tree, and greeted Adam and Eve with fair words that were full of deceit.

3 But when Adam and Eve saw their pleasant expression, and heard their sweet speech, Adam rose, welcomed them, and brought them to Eve, and they remained all together; Adam's heart the while, being glad because he thought concerning them, that they were the same angels, who had brought him gold, incense, and myrrh.

4 Because, when they came to Adam the first time, there came over him from them, peace and joy, through their bringing him good tokens; so Adam thought that they had come a second time to give him other tokens for him to rejoice therewith. For he did not know it was Satan; therefore he received them with joy and consorted with them.

5 Then Satan, the tallest of them, said, "Rejoice, O Adam, and be glad. Look, God has sent us to you to tell you something."

6 And Adam said, "What is it?" Then Satan answered, "It is a simple thing, yet it is the Word of God, will you accept it from us and do it? But if you will not accept it, we will return to God, and tell Him that you would not receive His Word."

7 And Satan said again to Adam, "Don't be afraid and don't tremble; don't you know us?"

8 But Adam said, "I do not know you."

9 Then Satan said to him, "I am the angel that brought you gold, and took it to the cave; this other angel is the one that brought you incense; and that third angel, is the one who brought you myrrh when you were on top of the mountain, and who carried you to the cave.

10 But as to the other angels our fellows, who bare you to the cave, God has not sent them with us this time; for He said to us, 'You will be enough'."

11 So when Adam heard these words he believed them, and said to these angels, "Speak the Word of God, that I may receive it."

12 And Satan said to him, "Swear, and promise me that you will receive it."

13 Then Adam said, "I do not know how to swear and promise."

14 And Satan said to him, "Hold out your hand, and put it inside my hand."

15 Then Adam held out his hand, and put it into Satan's hand; when Satan said to him, "Say, now—So true as God is living, rational, and speaking, who raised the stars in heaven, and established the dry ground on the waters, and has created me out of the four elements*, and out of the dust of the earth—I will not break my promise, nor renounce my word."

16 And Adam swore thus.

17 Then Satan said to him, "Look, it is now some time since you came out of the garden, and you know neither wickedness nor evil. But now God says to you, to take Eve who came out of your side, and to marry her so that she will bear you children, to comfort you, and to drive from you trouble and sorrow; now this thing is not difficult, neither is there any scandal in it to you.

* See the previous footnote in chapter XXXIV regarding the 'four elements'.

Chapter LXXI - Adam is troubled by the thought of marrying Eve.

1 But when Adam heard these words from Satan, he sorrowed much, because of his oath and of his promise, and said, "Shall I commit adultery with my flesh and my bones, and shall I sin against myself, for God to destroy me, and to blot me out from off the face of the earth?

2 Since, when at first, I ate of the tree, He drove me out of the garden into this strange land, and deprived me of my bright nature, and brought death over me. If, then, I should do this, He will cut off my life from the earth, and He will cast me into hell, and will plague me there a long time.

3 But God never spoke the words that you have said; and you are not God's angels, and you weren't sent from Him. But you are devils that have come to me under the false appearance of angels. Away from me; you cursed of God!"

4 Then those devils fled from before Adam. And he and Eve got up, and returned to the Cave of Treasures, and went into it.

5 Then Adam said to Eve, "If you saw what I did, don't tell anyone; for I sinned against God in swearing by His great name, and I have placed my hand another time into that of Satan." Eve, then, held her peace, as Adam told her.

6 Then Adam got up, and spread his hands before God, beseeching and entreating Him with tears, to forgive him what he had done. And Adam remained thus standing and praying forty days and forty nights. He neither ate nor drank until he dropped down on the ground from hunger and thirst.

7 Then God sent His Word to Adam, who raised him up from where he lay, and said to him, "O Adam, why have you sworn by My name, and why have you made agreement with Satan another time?"

8 But Adam cried, and said, "O God, forgive me, for I did this unwittingly; believing they were God's angels."

9 And God forgave Adam, saying to him, "Beware of Satan."

10 And He withdrew His Word from Adam.

11 Then Adam's heart was comforted; and he took Eve, and they went out of the cave, to prepare some food for their bodies.

12 But from that day Adam struggled in his mind about his marrying Eve; afraid that if he was to do it, God would be angry with him.

13 Then Adam and Eve went to the river of water, and sat on the bank, as people do when they enjoy themselves.

14 But Satan was jealous of them; and planned to destroy them.

Chapter LXXII - Adam's heart is set on fire. Satan appears as beautiful maidens.

1 Then Satan, and ten from his hosts, transformed themselves into maidens, unlike any others in the whole world for grace.

2 They came up out of the river in presence of Adam and Eve, and they said among themselves, "Come, we will look at the faces of Adam and Eve, who are of the men on earth. How beautiful they are, and how different is their look from our own faces." Then they came to Adam and Eve, and greeted them; and stood wondering at them.

3 Adam and Eve looked at them also, and wondered at their beauty, and said, "Is there, then, under us, another world, with such beautiful creatures as these in it?"

4 And those maidens said to Adam and Eve, "Yes, indeed, we are an abundant creation."

5 Then Adam said to them, "But how do you multiply?"

6 And they answered him, "We have husbands who have married us, and we bear them children, who grow up, and who in their turn marry and are married, and also bear children; and thus we increase. And if so be, O Adam, you will not believe us, we will show you our husbands and our children."

7 Then they shouted over the river as if to call their husbands and their children, who came up from the river, men and children; and every man came to his wife, his children being with him.

8 But when Adam and Eve saw them, they stood dumb, and wondered at them.

9 Then they said to Adam and Eve, "See all our husbands and our children? You should marry Eve, as we have married our husbands, so that you will have children as we have." This was a device of Satan to deceive Adam.

10 Satan also thought within himself, "God at first commanded Adam concerning the fruit of the tree, saying to him, 'Eat not of it; else of death you shall die.' But Adam ate of it, and

yet God did not kill him; He only decreed on him death, and plagues and trials, until the day he shall come out of his body.

11 Now, then, if I deceive him to do this thing, and to marry Eve without God's permission, God will kill him then."

12 Therefore Satan worked this apparition before Adam and Eve; because he sought to kill him, and to make him disappear from off the face of the earth.

13 Meanwhile the fire of sin came over Adam, and he thought of committing sin. But he restrained himself, fearing that if he followed this advice of Satan, God would put him to death.

14 Then Adam and Eve got up, and prayed to God, while Satan and his hosts went down into the river, in presence of Adam and Eve; to let them see that they were going back to their own world.

15 Then Adam and Eve went back to the Cave of Treasures, as they usually did; about evening time.

16 And they both got up and prayed to God that night. Adam remained standing in prayer, yet not knowing how to pray, by reason of the thoughts in his heart regarding his marrying Eve; and he continued so until morning.

17 And when light came up, Adam said to Eve, "Get up, let us go below the mountain, where they brought us gold, and let us ask the Lord concerning this matter."

18 Then Eve said, "What is that matter, O Adam?"

19 And he answered her, "That I may request the Lord to inform me about marrying you; for I will not do it without His permission or else He will make us perish, you and me. For those devils have set my heart on fire, with thoughts of what they showed us, in their sinful apparitions.

20 Then Eve said to Adam, "Why need we go below the mountain? Let us rather stand up and pray in our cave to God, to let us know whether this counsel is good or not."

21 Then Adam rose up in prayer and said, "O God, you know that we transgressed against you, and from the moment we transgressed, we were stripped of our bright nature; and our body became brutish, requiring food and drink; and with animal desires.

22 Command us, O God, not to give way to them without Your permission, for fear that You will turn us into nothing. Because if you do not give us permission, we shall be overpowered, and follow that advice of Satan; and You will again make us perish.

23 If not, then take our souls from us; let us be rid of this animal lust. And if You give us no order respecting this thing, then sever Eve from me, and me from her; and place us each far away from the other.

24 Then again, O God, if You separate us from each other, the devils will deceive us with their apparitions that resemble us, and destroy our hearts, and defile our thoughts towards

each other. Yet if it is not each of us towards the other, it will, at all events, be through their appearance when the devils come to us in our likeness." Here Adam ended his prayer.

Chapter LXXIII - The marriage of Adam and Eve.

1 Then God considered the words of Adam that they were true, and that he could long await His order, respecting the counsel of Satan.

2 And God approved Adam in what he had thought concerning this, and in the prayer he had offered in His presence; and the Word of God came to Adam and said to him, "O Adam, if only you had had this caution at first, before you came out of the garden into this land!"

3 After that, God sent His angel who had brought gold, and the angel who had brought incense, and the angel who had brought myrrh to Adam, that they should inform him respecting his marriage to Eve.

4 Then those angels said to Adam, "Take the gold and give it to Eve as a wedding gift, and promise to marry her; then give her some incense and myrrh as a present; and be you, you and she, one flesh."

5 Adam obeyed the angels, and took the gold and put it into Eve's bosom in her garment; and promised to marry her with his hand.

6 Then the angels commanded Adam and Eve to get up and pray forty days and forty nights; when that was done, then Adam was to have sexual intercourse with his wife; for then this would be an act pure and undefiled; so that he would have children who would multiply, and replenish the face of the earth.

7 Then both Adam and Eve received the words of the angels; and the angels departed from them.

8 Then Adam and Eve began to fast and pray, until the end of the forty days; and then they had sexual intercourse, as the angels had told them. And from the time Adam left the garden until he wedded Eve, were two hundred and twenty-three days, that is seven months and thirteen days.

9 Thus was Satan's war with Adam defeated.

Chapter LXXIV - The birth of Cain and Luluwa. Why they received those names.

1 And they lived on the earth working in order to keep their bodies in good health; and they continued so until the nine months of Eve's pregnancy were over, and the time drew near when she must give birth.

2 Then she said to Adam, "The signs placed in this cave since we left the garden indicate that this is a pure place and we will be praying in it again some time. It is not appropriate then, that I should give birth in it. Let us instead go to the sheltering rock cave that was formed by the command of God when Satan threw a big rock down on us in an attempt to kill us with it.

3 Adam then took Eve to that cave. When the time came for her to give birth, she strained a lot. Adam felt sorry, and he was very worried about her because she was close to death and the words of God to her were being fulfilled: "In suffering shall you bear a child, and in sorrow shall you bring forth a child."

4 But when Adam saw the distress in which Eve was, he got up and prayed to God, and said, "O Lord, look at me with the eye of Your mercy, and bring her out of her distress."

5 And God looked at His maid-servant Eve, and delivered her, and she gave birth to her first-born son, and with him a daughter.

6 The Adam rejoiced at Eve's deliverance, and also over the children she had borne him. And Adam ministered to Eve in the cave, until the end of eight days; when they named the son Cain, and the daughter Luluwa.

7 The meaning of Cain is "hater," because he hated his sister in their mother's womb; before they came out of it. Therefore Adam named him Cain.

8 But Luluwa means "beautiful," because she was more beautiful than her mother.

9 Then Adam and Eve waited until Cain and his sister were forty days old, when Adam said to Eve, "We will make an offering and offer it up in behalf of the children."

10 And Eve said, "We will make one offering for the first-born son and then later we shall make one for the daughter."

Chapter LXXV - The family revisits the Cave of Treasures. Birth of Abel and Aklia.

1 Then Adam prepared an offering, and he and Eve offered it up for their children, and brought it to the altar they had built at first.

2 And Adam offered up the offering, and asked God to accept his offering.

3 Then God accepted Adam's offering, and sent a light from heaven that shown on the offering. Adam and his son drew near to the offering, but Eve and the daughter did not approach it.

4 Adam and his son were joyful as they came down from on the altar. Adam and Eve waited until the daughter was eighty days old, then Adam prepared an offering and took it to Eve and to the children. They went to the altar, where Adam offered it up, as he was accustomed, asking the Lord to accept his offering.

5 And the Lord accepted the offering of Adam and Eve. Then Adam, Eve, and the children, drew near together, and came down from the mountain, rejoicing.

6 But they returned not to the cave in which they were born; but came to the Cave of Treasures, in order that the children should go around in it, and be blessed with the tokens brought from the garden.

7 But after they had been blessed with these tokens, they went back to the cave in which they were born.

8 However, before Eve had offered up the offering, Adam had taken her, and had gone with her to the river of water, in which they threw themselves at first; and there they washed themselves. Adam washed his body and Eve hers also clean, after the suffering and distress that had come over them.

9 But Adam and Eve, after washing themselves in the river of water, returned every night to the Cave of Treasures, where they prayed and were blessed; and then went back to their cave, where their children were born.

10 Adam and Eve did this until the children had been weaned. After they were weaned, Adam made an offering for the souls of his children in addition to the three times every week he made an offering for them.

11 When the children were weaned, Eve again conceived, and when her pregnancy came to term, she gave birth to another son and daughter. They named the son Abel and the daughter Aklia.

12 Then at the end of forty days, Adam made an offering for the son, and at the end of eighty days he made another offering for the daughter, and treated them, as he had previously treated Cain and his sister Luluwa.

13 He brought them to the Cave of Treasures, where they received a blessing, and then returned to the cave where they were born. After these children were born, Eve stopped having children.

Chapter LXXVI - Cain becomes jealous of Abel because of his sisters.

1 And the children began to grow stronger and taller; but Cain was hard-hearted, and ruled over his younger brother.

2 Often when his father made an offering, Cain would remain behind and not go with them, to offer up.

3 But, as to Abel, he had a meek heart, and was obedient to his father and mother. He frequently moved them to make an offering, because he loved it. He prayed and fasted a lot.

4 Then came this sign to Abel. As he was coming into the Cave of Treasures, and saw the golden rods, the incense and the myrrh, he asked his parents, Adam and Eve, to tell him about them and asked, "Where did you get these from?"

5 Then Adam told him all that had befallen them. And Abel felt deeply about what his father told him.

6 Furthermore his father, Adam, told him of the works of God, and of the garden. After hearing that, Abel remained behind after his father left and stayed the whole of that night in the Cave of Treasures.

7 And that night, while he was praying, Satan appeared to him under the figure of a man, who said to him, "You have frequently moved your father into making offerings, fasting and praying, therefore I will kill you, and make you perish from this world."

8 But as for Abel, he prayed to God, and drove away Satan from him; and did not believe the words of the devil. Then when it was day, an angel of God appeared to him, who said to him, "Do not cut short either fasting, prayer, or offering up an offering to your God. For, look, the Lord had accepted your prayer. Be not afraid of the figure which appeared to you in the night, and who cursed you to death." And the angel departed from him.

9 Then when it was day, Abel came to Adam and Eve, and told them of the vision he had seen. When they heard it, they grieved much over it, but said nothing to him about it; they only comforted him.

10 But as to the hard-hearted Cain, Satan came to him by night, showed himself and said to him, "Since Adam and Eve love your brother Abel so much more than they love you, they wish to join him in marriage to your beautiful sister because they love him. However, they wish to join you in marriage to his ugly sister, because they hate you.

11 Now before they do that, I am telling you that you should kill your brother. That way your sister will be left for you, and his sister will be cast away."

12 And Satan departed from him. But the devil remained behind in Cain's heart, and frequently aspired to kill his brother.

Chapter LXXVII - Cain, 15 years old, and Abel 12 years old, grow apart.

1 But when Adam saw that the older brother hated the younger, he endeavored to soften their hearts, and said to Cain, "O my son, take of the fruits of your sowing and make an offering to God, so that He might forgive you for your wickedness and sin."

2 He said also to Abel, "Take some of your sowing and make an offering and bring it to God, so that He might forgive you for your wickedness and sin."

3 Then Abel obeyed his father's voice, took some of his sowing, and made a good offering, and said to his father, Adam, "Come with me and show me how to offer it up."

4 And they went, Adam and Eve with him, and they showed him how to offer up his gift on the altar. Then after that, they stood up and prayed that God would accept Abel's offering.

5 Then God looked at Abel and accepted his offering. And God was more pleased with Abel than with his offering, because of his good heart and pure body. There was no trace of guile in him.

6 Then they came down from the altar, and went to the cave in which they lived. But Abel, by reason of his joy at having made his offering, repeated it three times a week, after the example of his father Adam.

7 But as to Cain, he did not want to make an offering, but after his father became very angry, he offered up a gift once. He took the smallest of his sheep for an offering and when he offered it up, his eyes were on the lamb.

8 Therefore God did not accept his offering, because his heart was full of murderous thoughts.

9 And they all thus lived together in the cave in which Eve had brought forth, until Cain was fifteen years old, and Abel twelve years old.

Chapter LXXVIII - Jealousy overcomes Cain. He makes trouble in the family. How the first murder was planned.

1 Then Adam said to Eve, "Behold the children are grown up; we must think of finding wives for them."

2 Then Eve answered, "How can we do it?"

3 Then Adam said to her, "We will join Abel's sister in marriage to Cain, and Cain's sister to Abel.

4 The said Eve to Adam, "I do not like Cain because he is hard-hearted; but let them stay with us until we offer up to the Lord in their behalf."

5 And Adam said no more.

6 Meanwhile Satan came to Cain in the figure of a man of the field, and said to him, "Behold Adam and Eve have taken counsel together about the marriage of you two; and they have agreed to marry Abel's sister to you, and your sister to him.

7 But if it was not that I love you, I would not have told you this thing. Yet if you will take my advice, and obey me, I will bring to you on your wedding day beautiful robes, gold and silver in plenty, and my relations will attend you."

8 Then Cain said with joy, "Where are your relations?"

9 And Satan answered, "My relations are in a garden in the north, where I once meant to bring your father Adam; but he would not accept my offer.

10 But you, if you will receive my words and if you will come to me after your wedding, you shall rest from the misery in which you are; and you shall rest and be better off than your father Adam."

11 At these words of Satan Cain opened his ears, and leaned towards his speech.

12 And he did not remain in the field, but he went to Eve, his mother, and beat her, and cursed her, and said to her, "Why are you planning to take my sister to wed her to my brother? Am I dead?"

13 His mother, however, quieted him, and sent him to the field where he had been.

14 Then when Adam came, she told him of what Cain had done.

15 But Adam grieved and held his peace, and said not a word.

16 Then on the next morning Adam said to Cain his son, "Take of your sheep, young and good, and offer them up to your God; and I will speak to your brother, to make to his God an offering of corn."

17 They both obeyed their father Adam, and they took their offerings, and offered them up on the mountain by the altar.

18 But Cain behaved haughtily towards his brother, and shoved him from the altar, and would not let him offer up his gift on the altar; but he offered his own on it, with a proud heart, full of guile, and fraud.

19 But as for Abel, he set up stones that were near at hand, and on that, he offered up his gift with a heart humble and free from guile.

20 Cain was then standing by the altar on which he had offered up his gift; and he cried to God to accept his offering; but God did not accept it from him; neither did a divine fire come down to consume his offering.

21 But he remained standing over against the altar, out of humor and meanness, looking towards his brother Abel, to see if God would accept his offering or not.

22 And Abel prayed to God to accept his offering. Then a divine fire came down and consumed his offering. And God smelled the sweet savor of his offering; because Abel loved Him and rejoice in Him.

23 And because God was well pleased with him, He sent him an angel of light in the figure of a man who had partaken of his offering, because He had smelled the sweet savor of his offering, and they comforted Abel and strengthened his heart.

24 But Cain was looking on all that took place at his brother's offering, and was angry because of it.

25 Then he opened his mouth and blasphemed God, because He had not accepted his offering.

26 But God said to cain, "Why do you look sad? Be righteous, that I may accept your offering. Not against Me have you murmured, but against yourself.

27 And God said this to Cain in rebuke, and because He abhorred him and his offering.

28 And Cain came down from the altar, his color changed and with a sad face, and came to his father and mother and told them all that had befallen him. And Adam grieved much because God had not accepted Cain's offering.

29 But Abel came down rejoicing, and with a gladsome heart, and told his father and mother how God had accepted his offering. And they rejoiced at it and kissed his face.

30 And Abel said to his father, "Because Cain shoved me from the altar, and would not allow me to offer my gift on it, I made an altar for myself and offered my gift on it."

31 But when Adam heard this he was very sorry, because it was the altar he had built at first, and on which he had offered his own gifts.

32 As to Cain, he was so resentful and so angry that he went into the field, where Satan came to him and said to him, "Since your brother Abel has taken refuge with your father Adam, because you shoved him from the altar, they have kissed his face, and they rejoice over him, far more than over you."

33 When Cain heard these words of Satan, he was filled with rage; and he let no one know. But he was laying wait to kill his brother, until he brought him into the cave, and then said to him:—

34 "O brother, the country is so beautiful, and there are such beautiful and pleasurable trees in it, and charming to look at! But brother, you have never been one day in the field to take your pleasure in that place.

35 Today, O, my brother, I very much wish you would come with me into the field, to enjoy yourself and to bless our fields and our flocks, for you are righteous, and I love you much, O my brother! But you have alienated yourself from me."

36 Then Abel consented to go with his brother Cain into the field.

37 But before going out, Cain said to Abel, "Wait for me, until I fetch a staff, because of wild beasts."

38 Then Abel stood waiting in his innocence. But Cain, the forward, fetched a staff and went out.

39 And they began, Cain and his brother Abel, to walk in the way; Cain talking to him, and comforting him, to make him forget everything.

Chapter LXXIX - A wicked plan is carried to a tragic conclusion. Cain is frightened. "Am I my brother's keeper?" The seven punishments. Peace is shattered.

1 And so they went on, until they came to a lonely place, where there were no sheep; then Abel said to Cain, "Behold, my brother, we are tired from walking; for we see none of the trees, nor of the fruits, nor of the flourishing green plants, nor of the sheep, nor any one of the things of which you told me. Where are those sheep of thine you told me to bless?"

2 Then Cain said to him, "Come on, and you shall see many beautiful things very soon, but go before me, until I catch up to you."

3 Then went Abel forward, but Cain remained behind him.

4 And Abel was walking in his innocence, without guile; not believing his brother would kill him.

5 Then Cain, when he came up to him, comforted him with his talk, walking a little behind him; then he ran up to him and beat him with the staff, blow after blow, until he was stunned.

6 But when Abel fell down on the ground, seeing that his brother meant to kill him, he said to Cain, "O, my brother, have pity on me. By the breasts we have sucked, don't hit me! By the womb that bore us and that brought us into the world, don't beat me to death with that staff! If you will kill me, take one of these large stones and kill me outright."

7 Then Cain, the hard-hearted, and cruel murderer, took a large stone, and beat his brother's head with it, until his brains oozed out, and he wallowed in his blood, before him.

8 And Cain repented not of what he had done.

9 But the earth, when the blood of righteous Abel fell on it, trembled, as it drank his blood, and would have destroyed Cain because of it.

10 And the blood of Abel cried mysteriously to God, to avenge him of his murderer.

11 Then Cain began at once to dig the ground wherein to lay his brother; for he was trembling from the fear that came over him, when he saw the earth tremble on his account.

12 He then cast his brother into the pit he made, and covered him with dust. But the ground would not receive him; but it threw him up at once.

13 Again Cain dug the ground and hid his brother in it; but again the ground threw him up on itself; until three times the ground thus threw up on itself the body of Abel.

14 The muddy ground threw him up the first time, because he was not the first creation; and it threw him up the second time and would not receive him, because he was righteous and good, and was killed without a cause; and the ground threw him up the third time and would not receive him, that there might remain before his brother a witness against him.

15 And so the earth mocked Cain, until the Word of God, came to him concerning his brother.

16 Then was God angry, and much displeased at Abel's death; and He thundered from heaven, and lightnings went before Him, and the Word of the Lord God came from heaven to Cain, and said to him, "Where is Abel your brother?"

17 Then Cain answered with a proud heart and a gruff voice, "How, O God? Am I my brother's keeper?"

18 Then God said to Cain, "Cursed be the earth that has drunk the blood of Abel your brother; and as for you, you will always be trembling and shaking; and this will be a mark on you so that whoever finds you, will kill you."

19 But Cain cried because God had said those words to him; and Cain said to Him, "O God, whosoever finds me shall kill me, and I shall be blotted out from the face of the earth."

20 Then God said to Cain, "Whoever finds you will not kill you;" because before this, God had been saying to Cain, "I shall put seven punishments on anyone that kills Cain." For as to the word of God to Cain, "Where is your brother?" God said it in mercy for him, to try and make him repent.

21 For if Cain had repented at that time, and had said, "O God, forgive me my sin, and the murder of my brother," God would then have forgiven him his sin.

22 And as to God saying to Cain, "Cursed be the ground that has drunk the blood of your brother." That also, was God's mercy on Cain. For God did not curse him, but He cursed the ground; although it was not the ground that had killed Abel, and committed a wicked sin.

23 For it was fitting that the curse should fall on the murderer; yet in mercy did God so manage His thoughts as that no one should know it, and turn away from Cain.

24 And He said to him, "Where is your brother?" To which he answered and said, "I know not." Then the Creator said to him, "Be trembling and quaking."

25 Then Cain trembled and became terrified; and through this sign did God make him an example before all the creation, as the murderer of his brother. Also did God bring trembling and terror over him, that he might see the peace in which he was at first, and see also the trembling and terror he endured at the last; so that he might humble himself before God, and repent of his sin, and seek the peace that he enjoyed at first.

26 And in the word of God that said, "I will put seven punishments on anyone who kills Cain," God was not seeking to kill Cain with the sword, but He sought to make him die of fasting, and praying and crying by hard rule, until the time that he was delivered from his sin.

27 And the seven punishments are the seven generations during which God awaited Cain for the murder of his brother.

28 But as to Cain, ever since he had killed his brother, he could find no rest in any place; but went back to Adam and Eve, trembling, terrified, and defiled with blood. . . .

Note from the Editor

Odin's Library Classics strives to bring you unedited and unabridged works of classical literature. As such, this is the complete and unabridged version of the original English text unless noted. In some instances, obvious typographical errors have been corrected. This is done to preserve the original text as much as possible. The English language has evolved since the writing and some of the words appear in their original form, or at least the most commonly used form at the time. This is done to protect the original intent of the author. If at any time you are unsure of the meaning of a word, please do your research on the etymology of that word. It is important to preserve the history of the English language.

Taylor Anderson

Manufactured by Amazon.ca
Bolton, ON